Aspects of Provence

James Pope-Hennessy was born in London in 1916 and educated at Downside and Balliol College, Oxford. He published his first book *London Fabric*, winner of the Hawthornden Prize, at the age of twenty-one. This was followed by biographies of Richard Monckton Milnes and of his son Lord Crewe, the Liberal statesman, as well as by travel books such as *America is an Atmosphere*, *Aspects of Provence*, first published in 1952, and *The Baths of Absalom*. In 1959 he published his bestselling biography of Queen Mary, a royal commission. He also wrote *Verandah: Some Episodes in the Crown Colonies 1867–1889*, *Sins of the Fathers*, a detailed study of the Atlantic slave-traders, a life of Robert Louis Stevenson, and a highly acclaimed biography of *Anthony Trollope*, which won the Whitbread Award for 1971 and is published in the Penguin Literary Biographies series.

James Pope-Hennessy died in 1974.

JAMES POPE-HENNESSY

ASPECTS
OF PROVENCE

PENGUIN BOOKS

PENGUIN BOOKS

Published by the Penguin Group
Penguin Books Ltd, 27 Wrights Lane, London W8 5TZ, England
Penguin Books USA Inc., 375 Hudson Street, New York, New York 10014, USA
Penguin Books Australia Ltd, Ringwood, Victoria, Australia
Penguin Books Canada Ltd, 2801 John Street, Markham, Ontario, Canada L3R 1B4
Penguin Books (NZ) Ltd, 182–190 Wairau Road, Auckland 10, New Zealand

Penguin Books Ltd, Registered Offices: Harmondsworth, Middlesex, England

First published by Longmans, Green 1952
Published in Penguin Books 1988
3 5 7 9 10 8 6 4 2
Map by Reginald Piggott

Printed in England by Clays Ltd, St Ives plc
Filmset in 10/12 Photina

TO
MAURICE GENDRON

CONTENTS

CHAPTER TEN
148

INDEX
157

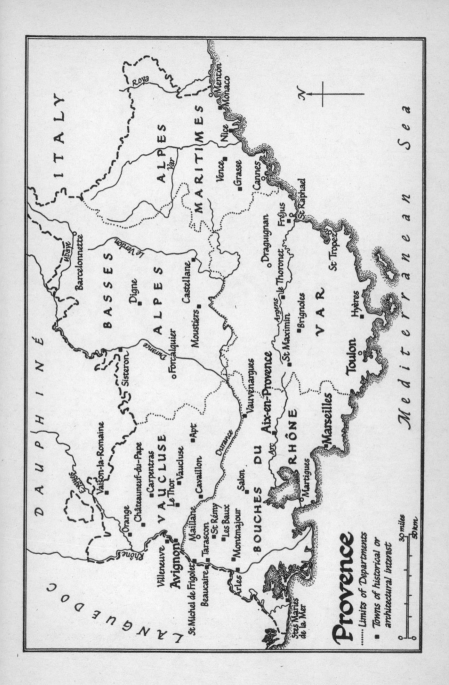

ITALY

Roya

Menton
Monaco

ALPES

Var

MARITIMES

Vence
Grasse
Nice

Cannes

St Raphael

DAUPHINÉ

Ubaye

Barcelonnette

Le Verdon

BASSES

Digne

ALPES

Castellane

Forcalquier

Moustiers

Durance

Sisteron

Dragugnan
o

Fréjus

le Thoronet

St Tropez

Argens

St Maximin

VAR

Brignoles

Vaison-la-Romaine

Carpentras

VAUCLUSE

Le Thor

Vaucluse

Apt

Durance

Vauvenargues

Aix-en-Provence

DU

Toulon
o

Hyères

Châteauneuf-du-Pape

Orange

Cavaillon

BOUCHES

RHÔNE

Marseilles

Rhône

Maillane

St Rémy

Salon

Martigues

Villeneuve

Tarascon

Les Baux

Avignon

Montmajour

Beaucaire

St Michel de Frigolet

Arles

LANGUEDOC

Stes Maries
de la Mer

Mediterranean Sea

N

Provence

.... Limits of Departments

■ Towns of historical or
  architectural interest

30 miles

50 km

FOREWORD

WHEN THIS BOOK FIRST APPEARED in 1952 I see that I described it as 'the outcome of notes made and impressions received during nine visits to Provence over the last five years'. I also emphasized that it was clearly not designed to replace the indispensable *Guide Bleu* on Provence in the Hachette series, nor to supplant the best and most exhaustive English work on the subject, Sir Theodore Andrea Cook's *Old Provence* (1905).

Since the book is concerned with certain unchanging aspects of Provence – monuments and landscapes – as well as with the experiences of earlier travellers through the region, I have not thought it requisite to revise the text. There are, however, noticeable differences between the Provence of today and that of a decade ago. Chief amongst these has been the massive resettlement of two hundred and thirty-eight thousand repatriated Frenchmen from Algeria. The dense concentration of most of these in the Marseilles–Aix area has changed the tempo of life in that part of Provence. The suburbs of Aix have been much enlarged; the repatriates have replaced the Dominicans at Saint-Maximin-la-Sainte-Baume; and, at Les Baux, commercialism has now finally proved that even ruins can be ruined.

I should, meanwhile, like to correct one signal error which has been pointed out to me. This is my tentative attribution of a strange stone bust in the grounds of the lunatic asylum of Saint-Paul in Saint-Rémy to 'some talented former inmate' of the institution. I have since learned that it is the work of Monsieur Thoret, a local sculptor, who has described it to me as an exact portrait of 'a degenerate Italian mimosa farmer in the mountains of the Estérel'. *Aspects of Provence* may indeed contain other errors, but since I have not been notified of these they remain, alas, impossible for me to correct.

J.P.-H.
1964

CHAPTER ONE

I

IN SEPTEMBER 1834, PROSPER MÉRIMÉE made his first visit to
Avignon. He had come down the Rhône by steamboat, and as he
stepped on to the quay and gazed about him, he felt that his river
journey had brought him to a foreign country. Nothing here
reminded him of France. The gay and sensual atmosphere of Avignon
seemed to him Valencian or Andalusian but not French. The olive
trees and the rose trees on the Rhône banks, the crenellated walls of
Avignon, the thick *patois* of the people, the curtains hung before the
shop doors, the swarthy working youths asleep at midday in the
streets – none of these things accorded with Mérimée's idea, or his
experience, of France. As he travelled through Provence on his
official task of inspecting its architectural monuments, reporting back
to his Minister in Paris, Mérimée's earliest impressions were confirmed. He realized that, independent from the fall of the Roman
Empire until united to the French crown in 1486, Provence differs
spiritually as well as visually from the rest of France. Like his friend
Henri Beyle, Mérimée compiled a little book of travel notes describing
what he had seen in this first journey through the backlands of the
Midi. Unlike Beyle, he lived to see maritime Provence requisitioned
as a health resort by ailing foreigners. He became as regular an
annual visitor to Lord Brougham's Cannes as any pale Victorian
invalid. He died there in the year 1870 and lies buried in the Protestant cemetery, a medallion profile portrait above his tomb.

Mérimée's *Notes d'un voyage dans le Midi de la France*,* which have
never been republished, remain of use and interest today. At the
period in which he and Beyle were travelling through Provence,

---

Notes d'un voyage dans le Midi de la France, par Prosper Mérimée, Inspecteur-
Général des Monuments de France. Published in Paris and Brussels, 1835. See also
the first volume of M. Maurice Parturier's edition of Mérimée's letters (Paris, Le Divan,
1941–8).

both were in some sense pioneers. To educated travellers of the eighteenth century, south and south-eastern France had seemed little more than a rather uncomfortable corridor to Italy. Towns like Aix and Avignon had been no more than staging-places on the route to Genoa and Florence. English travellers, when Europe was again open to them after the Napoleonic wars, were as usual the most adventurous; a few of them would make romantic detours to gape up at the Arles arena or to peer down into Petrarch's brackish fountain at Vaucluse.

In 1828, for instance, Lord and Lady Blessington, with six servants and three carriages, proceeded from Nîmes, where they had admired the Maison Carrée ('I should like to have a small model of it executed in silver, as an ornament for the centre of a table,' noted Lady Blessington*), to Arles, by way of Tarascon and Beaucaire. At the hotel at Arles – 'a large, crazy, old mansion, reminding me of some of those at Shrewsbury' – the *patronne*, in Arlesian dress, explained that her house was only frequented by farmers and their wives and daughters on fête days, and was seldom visited otherwise, save by an occasional traveller come to explore the antiquities. When the Blessingtons had finished luncheon, they found that several of the 'female neighbours' of the hostess had collected to admire the strangers – they 'gazed at us with as much surprise as if we were natives of Otaheite, beheld for the first time'. 'The people stared at us like savages,' wrote Lord FitzHarris† in his diary during a tour into Provence with his French wife in the spring of 1832. 'We hired a carriage to go to the Vaucluse, quite equal in beauty and curiosity to our expectations, and to its rich traditions,' he wrote a few days later . . . 'Our return to Avignon very disagreeable in an open carriage with a furious mistral which had risen suddenly since morning. The dust penetrated even into my writing-desk.' 'So far as civilization goes, this is a sad country,' we find in a letter from Mérimée to his friend Sutton Sharpe, dated from Avignon, 'and instead of Constitutions what these people badly need is a tyrant who would make

*The first three chapters of The Idler in France by the Countess of Blessington (Colburn, 1841) gives an account of the Blessingtons' progress from Nîmes to Lyons.

†Memoirs of an Ex-minister, by the Earl of Malmesbury (Longmans, Green, 1884), volume 1. Lord Malmesbury was again in Provence in May 1864, when he made the then rare expedition to Les Baux.

roads for them, and force them to keep themselves clean and to live better.' Travel in Provence is not, and never has been, all roses and orange-blossom, though the scents of both these flowers are wafted down the heat-locked streets of Avignon, and mingle with the smell of garlic, oil, bad drains and warm red wine.

With Lord Brougham's discovery of the beautiful bays of Cannes and La Napoule during the cholera epidemic of 1839 (when he was held in Provence by quarantine laws on his way to Genoa), it slowly dawned on English people that southern France could offer an alternative to Italy, and might even assuage that nostalgia for the Mediterranean which has since the sixteenth century been a constant theme in English life:

> 'Now give us lands where the olives grow,'
>   Cried the North to the South,
> 'Where the sun with a golden mouth can blow
> Blue bubbles of grapes down a vineyard-row!'
>   Cried the North to the South.

The last poem of Elizabeth Barrett Browning, written as she lay dying behind the Casa Guidi windows, forms a simple Victorian expression of this ancient English longing for the south.

In the forty years following Lord Brougham's invention of maritime Provence as a resort, rich English persons formed the habit of descending on its fishing-ports in ever-increasing crowds each early spring. Buying land in the hills behind these villages, they constructed for themselves palatial villas, protected by dark gardens designed to exclude the sun. But to these rich invaders as to their ancestors making the leisurely Grand Tour towards Italy, the whole of inland Provence, its hill-towns, its river-valleys and its sloping vineyards, remained unknown. Even towards the end of the last century the most obvious and unavoidable cities of Provence were being treated by these travellers as mere incidents of the southward journey – places with possible hotels and picturesque inhabitants, places you could glimpse from the railway-carriage window, and could rely on to give you a thrilling foretaste of pleasures to come. 'Libby's description of the rush into sunlight about Avignon,' wrote the eighth Duke of Argyll in 1874, in a letter very expressive of this casual, slightly insolent point of view, 'recalls the delight one always feels in the first sight, after an interval, of those delicious climes – delicious for a wee while,' the Duke cautiously added, 'for I confess I always weary of them after some time.'*

II

By the seventies and eighties of the last century, the present character of Cannes and the adjacent seacoast became well established. 'Cannes,' wrote Charles Lenthéric, the indispensable and erudite historian of maritime Provence, in 1880, 'is a town where you feel no need to work.'† The English residents, upon whom the natives skilfully and gladly battened, were either hedonists or invalids, and often both at once. They were in any case people of fashion and of money, members of a beau monde, and thus automatically incurious about their surroundings, so long as these permitted them to be both comfortable and effortlessly amused. They were not interested in the world that lay beyond their shady gardens, or the sheltered balconies of their hotels. They did not, for example, realize that the strange, secret valleys of the Côte des Maures, which the French called 'la Provence de la Provence', were superior in climate and far more lovely than the neighbourhood of La Bocca and of Cannes. Unwilling to risk their pony-traps and carriages on dubious, unknown roads, they were satisfied to visit each other's agreeable villas, and, if they wanted scenery, to drive up to some convenient vantage point such as the Buccleuchs' terrace at Garibondi with its statuary and its striped cactus plants, and its splendid vistas to the sea. Here they would sit, discussing lungs and anemones, the Duchess of Manchester or the English news. At their backs, as they gazed at the sea and the Estérel from the Duchess's gardens, stretched the whole fierce and mysterious country of Provence. For most of them this

*Letter of November 1874, to Sir J. McNeill, printed in Lady Frances Balfour's memoirs, *Ne Obliviscaris – Dinna forget.*

†Lenthéric, the author of a great two-volume work upon the river Rhône, was also author of three fascinating studies, all published by Plon, while anyone interested in Provence must read: *La Grèce et l'Orient en Provence* (1877), *Les Villes mortes du golfe de Lyon* (1879), and *La Provence maritime ancienne et moderne* (1880).

fact was of no moment. They did not dream of Forcalquier or Draguignan or Digne or Carpentras or Barcelonette, or Moustiers or
Vaison-la-Romaine, for they did not know of these, nor did they
know that the coast they had bedizened formed a mere bright rind to
an ancient independent county with a civilization more than two
thousand years old. Some of them might perhaps have glanced at
Augustus Hare's accounts of his diligent, adventurous expeditions
amongst the hills and valleys of the Vaucluse and the Var; but most
of the places he had visited seemed a long way from the coast, and
would surely have poor roads and worse hotels. Even the famous old
Hôtel de l'Europe at Avignon, today one of the most cosy and
agreeable in the world, was somewhat spartan a hundred years ago:
'This inn is thought one of the best in France and we appear to have
the best rooms yet bedrooms and sitting-room are of red tiles with
thin carpet over,' wrote John Stuart Mill the day before his wife's
death there in November 1858. Safe, cosseted, and well-served in
their villas, the rich compatriots of Hare would hardly feel inclined
to imitate his exploration of the hinterlands of High Provence. If they
thought of what lay behind them, they thought of an English winter
turning coldly to an English spring – of the carriage-horses slithering
on the rain-wet surfaces of Belgrave Square, of a crackling fire at
tea-time, in the long, dim library of some house in Lincolnshire.
Meanwhile, they were in the warmth, they were on the Mediterranean. Inhabitants of an infinitely luxurious cantonment, they
regarded themselves as staying on the French Riviera. They would
never have called it living in Provence.

Except for works of local or provincial scholarship – like the Abbé
Boze's volumes upon the town and church of Apt, published there in
the 1820s – few serious books were then available upon the architecture of Provence. In 1888 a Scots amateur of architecture, named
David MacGibbon, who had noticed this, produced a hefty volume
on the subject with the aim of drawing attention to the 'extraordinary variety and abundance of the ancient architectural monuments
of Provence'. He had been surprised to find how 'comparatively
unknown' the architectural wealth of Provence remained, although
it was not possible to go from England to the Riviera without passing
a good many Provençal châteaux, churches and Roman ruins on
your way. For much of his information, MacGibbon was driven to

rely on Mérimée's little survey, published half a century before; his book, illustrated by pencil sketches of small merit, is discursive in method and modest in aim. The places he described were chiefly obvious places, but it was the first large-scale attempt in English to make educated people conscious of the marvels of Provence. It was followed in 1905 by Sir Theodore Andrea Cook's invaluable two-volume work, *Old Provence*, a book which is unlikely to be superseded and which should be read and carried by every English person setting out to travel through Provence.

In the present century, a number of serious monographs in French, as well as several romanticized travel books, have dealt with the architecture of Provence. Certain sights have become perfectly familiar to tourists of every nationality – the staunch white walls of the papal palace at Avignon, the noble doorways of the private houses in the Cours Mirabeau at Aix, the tumbled ruins of Fréjus and the triumphal arch and open-air theatre at Orange. Certain rural areas have also become more famous and, so, more frequented – the Aix countryside, for instance, Le Tholonet and the Arc valley, with its heterogeneous collection of painters come to bask in Cézanne's sun. Yet, all the same, much of Provence remains happily unvisited. Do many strangers toil up to see the cavernous house fronts of Les Baux in the summer moonlight? Or penetrate into the fusty crypts of the Saintes-Maries-de-la-Mer, with its smell of gipsies' clothing? Or stroll out at evening through the flat vineyards round Saint-Maximin-la-Sainte-Baume? Or climb the hill above the abbey at Forcalquier to gaze down upon that strictly medieval landscape? Or stop to smell the lavender fields near Valensole? Or stare in spe-culation at the sugar-loaf rocks beside the Durance river at Les Mées? Or visit Barjols and its saw-mills in mid-January for the ceremony of the roasted ox? Or look down from the topmost tower of the château at Vaison on the cart-track that winds away through dull-grey olive groves to Buis-les-Baronnies?

III

In spite of certain magnificent churches and some world-famous Roman remains, Provence will never be as overrun with tourists as, say, Tuscany. Patently it has less to offer. The dingy municipal museums of Provençal towns are usually shut and seldom interesting. They contain a forest of plaster casts from Roman statues, but few excellent pictures or major works of art. The museums worth a visit can be counted on the fingers of two hands – the tapestry museum in the *archevêché* at Aix, the museum of painting in the same town, the Musée Calvet at Avignon, one of the two museums at Arles, the Musée Masséna at Nice, and so on. Nor is it a part of anybody's artistic education to see the second-rate basilica at Apt or the eighteenth-century Hôtel-Dieu at Carpentras. Provence, in fact, is a country for the amateur of travel – for those who feel a passionate interest in landscapes, towns, atmospheres, and human beings. Journeying from place to place through the rich Provençal scene, you are again and again impressed by the individuality of each tiny town in which you happen to spend a night. To try to analyse or to explain these contrasts is a perpetual temptation. Life at Forcalquier seems centred round the great abbey there; life at Saint-Maximin seems utterly detached from the immense Gothic basilica which stands at the edge of the town. Surely there must be some reason, or a whole set of reasons, why the pattern of Provençal life should be of a slightly different shape in every place? As an outsider you can only judge these questions in relation to yourself. From this viewpoint you find certain constants which recur throughout your journeys. The most immediately noticeable is the quality of your welcome in the little Provençal hotels.

I can think of few greater pleasures than to leave the neighbourhood of Cannes and to cross the Maritime Alps through Castellane to Digne, or to go north-westward through the foothills to Draguignan. You pass villages where swallows circle round some stalwart belfry crowned with an open cupola of iron.

You pass churches and small fortified houses perched on pinnacles of rock like something from a background by Patinir. You pass fields of heavy-faced sunflowers, their heads tilted to the ground, their yellow petals startling in the morning light. On arriving at your destination – or at some wayside place by which you feel beguiled, for these are not journeys to be made by plan – you open the door of a shuttered, silent hotel. The floors, and the wide shallow treads of the staircase, are of hexagonal red tiles, scrupulously beeswaxed.

Your room, which may look as though it was last slept in some fifty years ago, contains a huge squeaking bedstead with rough cotton sheets that smell of soap and river-water. The *patronne*, whose husband does the cooking, talks to you with a thick accent in a language which you cannot understand (nor does she understand much of your French). The chambermaid is gnarled and spectacled, the waiter, if there is one, young and debonair, with sailor's trousers and one or two gold teeth. The service is as slow as you could possibly imagine, but also as solicitous, and you eat pâtés of thrush or omelettes stuffed with brittle local truffles. As you lie in bed at night, behind the closed shutters, you simply cannot believe that Cannes – the Carlton terrace, the browning bodies on the beaches, the night-clubs and the bars – is just across the mountains. In fact you cannot believe that Cannes, or places like it, have any real existence at all. Beneath the window, the men and boys are playing a final game of bowls by lamplight. Their excited cries and the dry click-click of the bowls are the last things you hear as you fall asleep. This is the Provence which Monsieur Jean-Louis Vaudoyer has taught his compatriots to admire and understand.* This is the Provence certain aspects of which I should like to examine in this book.

---

*See J.-L. Vaudoyer's *Beautés de la Provence* and *Nouvelles Beautés de la Provence* (Bernard Grasset, 1926 and 1928). These desultory travel sketches are well worth reading.

CHAPTER TWO

I

AVIGNON IS IN EVERY WAY the antithesis to Aix-en-Provence. Aix is a sad and secret city. It is a composition of shadowy streets and moss-grown fountains, of old ladies dressed in black on long, late Sunday afternoons, of high, cold, echoing cafés only noisy in the university term. People in Aix walk quickly, but with discretion, while Avignon (like New Orleans) is one of those cities in which people look you in the eyes. In Avignon there are days on which everyone seems young and all the young seem beautiful.

When Mérimée was in Avignon he observed that most of the working men carried their coats upon one shoulder like a Spanish cloak. He found the people gallant, in their style and gait; one of the first things you notice about Avignon today is the quality and the tempo of the movement in the streets – the lithe hips, the springy stride, the way in which the bicyclists seem to float swiftly along the Rue de la République. This modern boulevard, driven from the railway station beyond the ramparts up to the Place Georges Clemenceau near the Palace of the Popes, has been much criticized, yet it has not changed the atmosphere of Avignon. You may modify the layout of an ancient city but you cannot alter its real character. An indolent but almost audible excitement throbs through this Rhône city. This excitement is not due to a sunny climate, for seething with heat in summer, by autumn Avignon is often damp and rain-swept. The mistral screams through the courtyards of the palace and through the stark branches of the plane trees near the Porte de l'Oulle where the sad, dark gipsies linger by their painted caravans.

The seat of the papacy from 1309 to 1379, Avignon was then notorious for the luxury of the life at the papal court, a luxury which radiated out from the Palace of the Popes and the mansions of the cardinals into every back street and alley of the city. The property of the papacy until the Treaty of Tolentino in 1797, Avignon retained throughout this period the tone set by the fourteenth-century popes and by the subsequent legates and vice-legates who ruled the city. Like the neighbouring papal dominions, the straggling Comtat Venaissin,* Avignon became the natural asylum for fugitives from France and farther countries. Exiles, plotters, murderers and criminals assembled there, adding both to the pleasures and the dangers of this hedonistic town. 'I cannot think there is a more agreeable place in this world than Avignon, where my husband's affairs detain me for some time,' wrote Madame Dunoyer in the later part of the reign of Louis Quatorze,

... the situation of this City is charming, the River Rhône bathes her walls, without them there is nothing seen but Meadows and Gardens, with Magnificent Buildings, within the Houses of Messieurs de Montréal and Crillon, are the most Beautiful can be seen ... Here are Convents of both Sexes, yet more to embellish this Inchanting City, which is under the clearest Sky, and the easiest Government imaginable, owning no authority but the Pope's, exercised by a Vice-legate, who is always a Man of Quality and very easie to live with; he at present is called Delfini, he is a very accomplished and noble Venetian ... every body is Rich, and all show an Air of Felicity ... Play, which may be called the universal Pleasure, is carried here as high as you please.†

But a few days later Madame Dunoyer was shocked to meet the Marquis de Ganges, who had fled from France after murdering his wife: and in another letter she reported the most recent scandal of the city – the castration and midnight murder of an amiable innkeeper by the Chevalier de Bouillon, and 'the most debauch'd youths of the town'. The legate Delfini, afraid of the Chevalier's relatives, could only order him to leave Avignon at once.

*The territory of the Comtat Venaissin, given to the Holy See by Raymond VII of Toulouse after the defeat of the Albigenses in 1229, was gradually enlarged in the fourteenth century until it extended as far north as Visan and Valréas. The principality of Orange and the town of Mondragon formed enclaves of independent territory in the papal dominions, but the papacy owned a few small towns outside the Comtat. Until 1320 Pernes was the capital of the Comtat Venaissin, and from then on the capital was Carpentras. Papal control of the Comtat ended in 1791.

†Letters from a Lady at Paris to a Lady at Avignon ... Written by Madam Du Noyer (London, 1716). This, the third English edition of Madame Dunoyer's Lettres galantes, has a preface defaming the authoress and referring to English interest in Avignon as the place of refuge for the Pretender.

A city can lose its habits no more than can an individual, and it is not surprising that Avignon is still known for its immorality and for sudden outbursts of crime, for these are as much a legacy of the easy-going papal rule as the palace itself, or as the great seventeenth-century hôtels in the Rue Banasterie and the Quartier des Fusteries.

Beautiful and carefree, Avignon is also a place in which the most sordid murders are committed, usually for motives of gain. Tourists who bowl out in their cars over the river and Île Barthelasse towards the biscuit-coloured village of Villeneuve-lès-Avignon, lying in the soft evening light that Corot caught, may not realize that swollen, softened corpses are sometimes found jammed against the piers of the road bridge, or fished out of the pebbly side-shallows of the Rhône. More even than the majority of Latin cities, Avignon has a dual character, a character of Jekyll and Hyde. Because it is an exceptionally lovely and intelligent city, it can be an exceptionally evil one as well.

II

I first saw Avignon at eight o'clock on an evening in early September. We had spent three days in coming leisurely down from Poitiers – down through the Limousin and into the Auvergne, where the houses in the towns have slate roofs, and the towns themselves are pale grey. We had seen the tall pink cathedral of Rodez standing upright in that uninspiring town. We had had a breakdown on a deserted heath outside Millau at nightfall, but the next day we had seen one of the most superb and astounding sights in the whole of France – the Romanesque abbey of Conques, clamped up above the Lot gorges amid the billowing autumn trees, and containing the shimmering gold reliquaries that have been there since they were made in the tenth century. We had come down the valley of the Hérault, an earthly paradise of tumbling crystal waterfalls, haphazard cottages and young green poplar trees. Then, quite suddenly, in latest afternoon, we had come out among the foothills and into the stiffened panorama of the Languedoc and Provence – a landscape that one felt to be classical and angular after the romantic valleys of the Hérault and the Lot. Here were cypresses standing rigidly in the warm windless air, cube-shaped houses with orange roofs, villages with high narrow streets, pointed hillocks capped by turreted churches and windowless farms. In the villages, fountains tinkled under plane trees, and men stood about in loose groups, playing bowls. We had driven on into the cypress-studded outskirts of Nîmes, where the pale bright houses set in their dark hedges make a pattern like embroidery. At Nîmes we had seen the swirling Louis Quinze gardens, designed on a bias, and so much more beautiful than the echoing, dust-laden Maison Carrée or the arena which, like many Roman ruins in Provence, seems somehow far too old. At Beaucaire we had first come upon the Rhône, that wide white river with its sand-drifts and tufted islands. On the opposite side of the river, near the castle of Tarascon, are the ruins of the church of Sainte-Marthe, destroyed in the war. We drove on by the light of a high magenta sunset, in which the screens of cypress trees looked black and thin. Suddenly we were in Avignon.

Entering the city by the Porte Saint-Michel, we were at once swept up into the evening animation of the streets. It was a festival week in Avignon, and they had hidden electric-light bulbs in the plane trees of the Cours Jean-Jaurés. After you have been some time in the city you begin to notice which parts of it have the finest *platanes*. There are the ranks of these trees, four deep, along the nearside of the river, beyond the ramparts. There are the twenty tall plane trees in the Place des Carmes, outside the church of Saint-Symphorien. There is the single giant tree in the courtyard of the Hôtel de l'Europe, justly famous for a hundred and fifty years. The little lights in the trees on that first evening in Avignon seemed to add a particular excitement to the arboreal aspect of the city. They made the silhouettes of the leaves and branches of the plane trees seem complicated and strange.

On the evening we arrived in Avignon, a French company was acting Shakespeare in the courtyard of the Palace of the Popes. The play was *Richard Deux*. The courtyard was floodlit. The acting was inferior. The general effect was good. The mistral, which had sprung up towards evening, blew in spirals in the courtyard, as though a part of it was trapped there and could not get out. It lifted the robes and draped medieval head-dresses of the actors, and made the spectators shiver on their wooden chairs. The translation of the play was pedestrian, uncut, and seemed as if it might go on for ever; but what was curious was the breathless fascination with which the audience watched the stage. Stripped of its English verse, the story of the play was crude, yet to these people of Avignon, and to these peasants and farmers from the country round, it seemed logical and sympathetic. I had in the past seen one or two other theatrical representations in Provençal towns, but I did not remember this minute, enthusiastic attention before. I suspected that this tale of medieval violence, murder and intrigue precisely suited the spectators.

III

It was in the previous year that I had first realized how much ferocity lurks in the Provençal character, and lies implicit in the landscape. Foreigners who race through it in the spring or summer to the coast are deceived into thinking Provence a smiling southern country, inhabited by a handsome and amiable race. These foreigners are wrong. Smiling, carefree, and extraordinarily amiable, the Provençaux are also passionately emotional. They are capable of considerable cruelty. When the mistral blows week after week over fields and vineyards, curling the tips of the black cypress trees, anything may happen in the towns and villages, the isolated farms and *cabanons*, of Provence. This was the moment, for example, at which a man put his wife in a barrel, and hurled it off the summit of Les Baux. This is the moment at which some unknown victim is trussed up and dropped quietly into the Rhône.

A few days before I left Paris on my first journey to Provence, I went to seek the advice of Gertrude Stein, who had spent a year in an hotel at Saint-Rémy, writing. It was about nine in the evening, a May evening, and as I walked across the Pont Neuf the chestnut trees on the Vert Galant were glittering in the twilight. When I entered her apartment in the Rue Christine, to the shrill sound of her poodle Basket's yapping, I found Miss Stein seated on her sofa before an empty fireplace, her hands on her knees. That calm, still room in which her powerful personality seemed to vie with that of the great ochre Picasso portrait of her on the wall, was lit by a solitary shaded lamp on the table at her back. Against this light her imperial head and lengthy, sensitive and somehow melancholy face were especially impressive. We talked first of a manuscript I had brought to show her, and then of the negro problem in the southern States. Presently we got on to the subject which I really wanted to inquire about – Provence. She said many things that seemed illuminating, and which I later found out by experience to be true as well. But the one piece of advice she gave me, and which I have since had many times reason to remember, was on the effects of the mistral, and of the Provençal landscape, upon oneself. 'You'll find you're getting nervous down there,' she warned me. 'You'll find you're suddenly having a terrific fight with your very greatest friend. Don't let that worry you. You just won't be able to help it.' She laughed.

Since that evening in Paris I have had many opportunities to learn she was right. People who seem tactful and affectionate in England are liable to become explosive in Provence. The explosion takes place quite unaccountably; it may equally happen in a gaunt hotel room at Arles or in a Victorian garden within reach of Cannes, but it always happens when it is least expected. The dangerous days are those on which the mistral is blowing, for this steady persistent wind seems to rip your self-control to tatters, and sear your nerves with a white-hot iron comb. Stendhal called the mistral 'the great drawback to all the pleasures that one can find in Provence'. 'When the mistral rules Provence,' he writes elsewhere in the *Mémoires d'un touriste*,* 'one does not know where to take refuge; there is in fact fine sunshine, but a cold, insupportable wind penetrates into the most carefully closed room, and aggravates the nerves to a degree which exasperates the very calmest people.'

The mistral also sweeps the coast of the French Riviera, where it is partially (but only partially) responsible for that phenomenon famous among foreign visitors – 'the south-of-France row'.

**Mémoires d'un touriste*, volume I, établissement du texte et préface par Henri Martineau (Paris, Le Divan, 1929).

Of the various ways by which I have entered Provence, that early autumn drive from Poitiers down to Avignon remains in my mind as the most instructive. The contrasted beauties of the scenery through which we travelled form a preface or a commentary to the very independent beauty of Provence. To cross the Rhône at evening and to penetrate the rampart gates of Avignon towards nightfall is anyway a mysterious, a dreamlike experience. Sometimes I have tried to decide which is the loveliest hour of the day in Provence. The choice would seem to lie between earliest morning, when even the dwarf shadows of the olive trees look elongated, and the rich short moments before sunset. I first saw Provence at dawn, through the dirty window of a third-class railway carriage, after a night of intermittent sleep.

There are few places in the world which seem interesting, let alone beautiful, under such circumstances. Tired, thirsty and grimy, I had awoken with a jolt, feeling as though my eyes had been torn out and incompetently replaced in their sockets. Putting a finger between the edge of the dusty blind and the woodwork of the carriage window, I peered languidly out. What I saw surprised me. It was just before sunrise, and there was a grey-white glare of curious intensity over the whole long landscape that was spinning by. Then, as I watched, the sun rose, and with it the whole panorama ceased looking like an under-exposed photograph and came literally to light – the cabin roofs shone orange, the fields turned out to be scattered with poppies of the colour of new blood, the long green grass was streaked with yellow flowers and cobalt flowers and round scabious flowers that were a hard, firm mauve. Over the distant crimson hills the sky was already blue, and the few people in the fields were a very dark walnut brown. Nothing I had expected of Provence had equalled the harsh and yet mysterious quality of this flying landscape. It was not at all a Lamartinian or a literary landscape. It would be almost impossible to remake it in words, I reflected. It was a painter's landscape wholly – a landscape for the brush, but better still a landscape for a palette-knife.

We got down from the train at Orange at seven o'clock. We went straight out into the street and across to a café behind some tall trees. A young-looking woman with a son who appeared to be ten years her senior gave us some coffee and some eggs. We then walked down the white, dusty road, between yellow garden walls mantled in red and white roses, to see the Roman theatre, which looked almost insufferably ancient in the fresh morning air. Near the theatre a fountain stood under a lime tree, and here we washed our faces and looked at the outside of the theatre again. This time it seemed easier to see. We then walked back to the station and boarded the train for Vaison-la-Romaine. From Orange to Vaison is twenty-seven kilometres, but to traverse this distance the train takes nearly two hours. It wandered along through the brilliant fields, stopping at five or six stations, drawing all the time nearer to the high foothills which still concealed the Mont Ventoux. Each of the three small, old-fashioned carriages had an open platform at either end, and we stood on one of these, waiting for Vaison to appear. After much meandering in and out of this dazzling landscape, the train headed suddenly for one of the hills. It seemed for a moment as though it would plunge into it, and that the hill would prove hollow like one in a northern folk-tale. But then, just as abruptly, the train switched to the right, dived between this hill and the next, and turned a curve. We saw Vaison-la-Romaine.

Vaison-la-Romaine consists of two towns. There is the *basse ville* built on the site of the Roman town, against a hillside in which an amphitheatre has lately been discovered. This town lies on the hither side of the Ouvèze, a low-flowing, jade-green river crossed by a simple Roman bridge. The *haute ville*, to which the inhabitants withdrew at the epoch of the barbarian invasions, clings to a lofty precipitous rock which is capped by the ruined square castle of the thirteenth-century Comtes de Toulouse. Both towns are dotted with plane trees, lime trees, cypress trees, and oleanders. There are also a few youngish poplars. In Paris we had been shown a post-card of the house we were going to stay in at Vaison. It was a small house built on the corner of the castle ramparts, high up above the old town, a modern version of a Roman villa, with arched windows and a plain tiled roof. As the train entered the station of Vaison one could immediately identify the house, far away on the other side of the Ouvèze, and perched upon a cliff of rock. It was called Les Arceaux.

There were no porters and no taxis. Putting our suitcases on a hand-cart, we set off to wheel this down the sloping tree-bordered road that leads from the station through the low town and across the Roman bridge. This shady road bordered by plane trees finds its counterpart in almost every small town in the Midi, but that walk down it has remained clearly in my mind. It seemed to be the road into Provence itself.

Once across the Ouvèze we toiled up to the *haute ville*, unlocking the wooden door in the garden wall of Les Arceaux with a big iron key given us in the town. The garden was waist high in weeds and grasses, and poppies, marguerites and ragged sorrel. At one end of the garden, opposite the terrace of the house, stood an unfinished circular tower built of rough-hewn blocks of stone. Close up against the side of this tower grew a pomegranate bush in full flower. This relentless colour, flaming between the white stones of the tower and the hard blue of the morning sky, is my first salient memory of these first hours in Provence. Since then I have noticed again and again that the strongest memories of Provence are colour memories. It is a country in which colour seems more important than form.

V

Until the final completion of the Paris–Marseilles railway line there were two usual ways of access to Provence. The traditional one was to go down the Rhône by boat from Lyons, a route which meant braving the narrow arches of the bridge at Pont Saint-Esprit, and which, as readers of Madame de Sévigné's letters will remember, was not considered invariably safe. The other was to travel along the uneven crowded road that wound upon the river's bank, through Valence, Montélimar, Caderousse and Avignon, whence you struck off via Cavaillon, Aix and Saint-Maximin for Toulon and Marseilles. The boat was quickest. 'Those who prefer the shortest routes, or who are in a hurry, embark upon the Rhône at Lyons to go down into Provence,' stated the compilers of a competent and typical two-volume road-book of France, published in Paris in 1724 and entitled *Nouveau Voyage de France avec un itinéraire et des cartes*. Those, on the other hand, who were travelling for sightseeing and instruction were told to go to Grenoble, and journey thence to Marseilles and to Toulon. For these inquisitive people, with plenty of time on their hands, the editors of the *Nouveau Voyage* had planned a whole itinerary from Paris to Marseilles by way of Grenoble which they cheerfully recommended as 'the longest, but also one of the most curious, journeys to be made in France', but at the same time they printed a map of the more logical road from Lyons to Valence. A stop in Aix was urged upon all but the hastiest travellers, since this was rated one of the French provincial towns best imitating Paris, 'both for the beauty of its buildings and the manners of its inhabitants'.

In the early summer of 1837, Stendhal, who intended to spend a fortnight in Provence, set out for Avignon from Lyons. Although he had just travelled by steamer down the Saône – a journey during which he had admired the water-meadows, read Shakespeare, and reflected upon the sublime character of Madame Roland (*'après ce grand caractère sont venues les dames de l'empire, qui pleuraient dans leur calèche au retour de Saint-Cloud, quand l'empereur avait trouvé leurs robes de mauvais goût'*) – Beyle did not at first think of going down the Rhône by the same means, but his experiences of the road from Lyons to Vienne and Valence, as well as the rude advice given him by a young man in the hotel at the last of these towns, persuaded him to embark upon the river. He was annoyed, though not of course surprised, that the Lyons–Vienne highway should follow the mountainous left bank of the Rhône, instead of the more level right bank of the river; and he was infuriated by the way in which his light *calèche* was almost smashed two or three times by the lumbering, six-horse carts and wagons which brought soap, oil, dried fruits, wine and barrels of anchovies northwards from Provence. The ascent of the Rhône was extremely dangerous, and the produce of Provence was still sent up to Paris and the northern cities by road. The carts and horses were in charge of huge Provençal wagoners, whose arrogant manners, uncertain tempers and long whips were the terror of all travellers. Stendhal, who later witnessed near Avignon the lashing of a child on a donkey by one of these brutal *rouliers de Provence*, found their behaviour on the road intolerable. He realized he could not protest as they pushed his *calèche* towards the ditch. '*Et, ce qu'il y a de pis pour un grand coeur, je n'aurais pu me venger,*' he commented, considering the possibility of an accident; '*le moindre signe d'insurrection de ma part m'aurait valu les coups de fouet de deux ou trois charretiers provençaux, les plus grossiers et les moins endurants du monde.*'

These same Provençal wagoners were great heroes and much respected in their own country. In *Mes Origines*, that haunting account of his Provençal childhood and youth, the poet Mistral records the reminiscences of Lamouroux, the wagoner who headed a caravan of pilgrims crossing the Camargue for the annual festival at the Saintes-Maries-de-la-Mer. The year was 1855, and many of the stories which Lamouroux told the young poet as the carts loaded with peasants and farm-people slowly wound their way from Avignon to Arles, dealt with a period already past. He said that he was speaking of the time before the railways had ruined the wagoners – '*Ah! messieurs, je vous parle de l'époque du roulage*' – and he described the welcome that used to await them at every inn on the road from Marseilles and Avignon to Paris, and how bravely the wagoners walked beside their horses, one hand on the bridle rein, in the other a whip. They were dressed in blue shirts, velvet breeches and gaiters. They wore coloured bonnets on their dark, curly heads. Their great woollen capes bellied out behind them in the wind. If all went well they sang songs as they marched along, and shouted greetings in Provençal to the other wagoners as they passed. But if things went awry, or a wagon going down refused to make room for one coming up, the result was a fight with whips and stones which often resulted in the death of one of the contestants: '*d'un coup de roulon, on vous decervelait l'homme*'. From Marseilles to Lyons the wagoners marched on the left of their beasts, but at Lyons this Provençal usage stopped, and they changed to the right. Everything else changed at Lyons, too, including the climate; the wagons would often continue northwards in ceaseless rain, over roads turned to a sea of mud. On the outskirts of Paris the wagoners' spirits rose again, and they would enter the city to the sound of cracking whips. Lamouroux declared gaily that the Parisians would put their hands to their ears as they heard it, crying out '*Allons! les Provençaux arrivent!*'

Is it any wonder that most people preferred to travel southwards by the boat?

The river Rhône has a quality of melancholy, for all its grandeur. I have never forgotten the impression made upon me, one March afternoon many years ago, when, at the age of fourteen, I set out from Villeneuve at the end of the lake of Geneva to walk across the Rhône valley towards the French frontier. It was a chilly day of melting snow. The valley seemed entirely empty. The Rhône flowed wide and white. Suddenly I came upon a very old, bearded fisherman, standing knee-deep in the river. I remember thinking that he seemed like a figure of Time or Death. It was an unbearably sad and lonely scene.

The same sadness – it is perhaps an attribute of all great rivers – can be sensed in the Rhône of the south, sweeping down between the sun-shot vineyards to Marseilles and the sea. It is an atmosphere which Mistral has reproduced in *Le Poème du Rhône*, the tragedy in twelve cantos in which he skilfully combined legend with reality – the old Provençal story of the Drac who inhabits the bed of the river and can adopt human form, with the description of daily life on board one of the old Rhône boats going southwards to the annual Foire de Beaucaire. Even seen through the veil of the French translation, this great work seems filled with the beauty of the Rhône banks and the gaiety of the boatmen and the songs sung by three Venetian ladies going to Avignon to seek their gold. The idyllic love of the young prince Guilhem d'Orange, whose beard is the colour of the yellow iris, and of l'Anglore, the girl who lives beside the Rhône, is doomed. On their return northwards from the fair the boat is wrecked and both of them are drowned. The melancholy of the river is constantly emphasized throughout the poem, and strays again and again across it like shadows on a day of sun. It is epitomized in the young prince's speech to the Venetian ladies, who have told him that their family has been living for generations upon the belief that their lost wealth lies buried in Avignon, near the Palace of the Popes. Guilhem d'Orange admires them for their illusion:

> *Et vous faites bien, parbleu! et fort bien,*
> *dit le jeune sage; car la vie, qu'est-elle?*
> *sinon un songe, une apparence au loin,*

une illusion sur l'eau glissante,
qui, devant nos yeux s'enfuyant toujours,
comme un jeu de miroir nous éblouit . . .

In several ways the mood of this fine poem forms an important introduction to Provence.

With the shooting of the bridge of the Saint-Esprit, the Rhône boats entered Provence. The bridge has twenty arches, each of them narrow. In the old days many accidents occurred, although intrepid English travellers thought the boatmen made an unjustified and theatrical fuss about the danger. Stendhal, who wondered that someone did not remove one of the piers so as to make a wider gap for boats, was told that timid clients could be put down before the bridge, and picked up again after it. In a characteristic paradox he remarked that these were in reality brave people to whom fear gave the courage to risk their fellow-passengers' contempt.

Stendhal was immediately receptive to the Rhône scenery: *'Je suis dans l'enchantment des rives du Rhône'*, he wrote on the steamboat on 12 June 1837, as they were moving slowly past Montélimar. It is indeed a wonderful journey. 'This journey by water is the only way to see the valley of the Rhône', Lord FitzHarris had noted five years earlier. '. . . Arrived at Avignon, at the Hôtel de l'Europe, after three days' enjoyment of the grandest scenery without the slightest fatigue. What a difference from the same journey, cramped in a carriage, and only half seeing one bank of this glorious river!' The FitzHarrises were rich and travelled in comfort. At Lyons they had hired a private boat for four hundred francs and put their carriages on it. This was an ideal way to see the Rhône, but the public steamboat, which swept along at twenty miles an hour, was not always so agreeable: 'a very dirty vessel full of merchandise, and with only three or four other passengers', wrote Dickens of it in *Pictures from Italy*.* With his wife, his sister-in-law and all his children, Dickens was on his way to Genoa, where he spent the year 1845–6. They had rolled across France in their great *berline*, and taken the steamboat for Marseilles at Lyons.

*Pictures from Italy, by Charles Dickens, vignette illustrations on wood by Samuel Palmer (Bradbury and Evans, 1846).

For the last two days we had seen great sullen hills, the first indications of the Alps, lowering in the distance. Now, we were rushing on beside them: sometimes close beside them: sometimes with an intervening slope, covered with vineyards. Villages and small towns hanging in mid-air, with great woods of olives seen through the light open towers of their churches, and clouds moving slowly on, upon the steep acclivity behind them; ruined castles perched on every eminence; and scattered houses in the clefts and gullies of the hills; made it very beautiful . . . There lay before us, that same afternoon, the broken bridge of Avignon, and all the city baking in the sun . . .'

In the phrase 'baking' Dickens seems fumbling after an image to convey the odd dry colour of the ramparts of Avignon, which Stendhal defines more crisply: 'Le temps a donné a ces pierres si égales, si bien jointes, d'un si beau poli, une teinte uniforme de feuille sèche qui en augmente la beauté.'

In the autumn of 1846, when the Dickenses were back home, another English literary party set off from Lyons down the Rhône. Mrs Anna Jameson, the art historian, working feverishly at a new book in Paris with her young niece Gerardine, had been astounded to be joined by Elizabeth Barrett, whom she had left an invalid on a sofa in Wimpole Street, and her bridegroom Robert Browning. Anxious not to miss a moment of this great romance, Mrs Jameson easily persuaded the Brownings that they should all travel down to Italy together. By the time they left Paris the autumn was drawing in, and by the time they reached Avignon the weather had definitely broken. Mrs Browning had been 'very suffering' and had fainted over and over again, forcing them to spend a complete day resting 'at some wretched place'. 'To complete the *tedium* of our progress,' wrote Mrs Jameson to her sister Charlotte Murphy,* 'we had incessant rain down the Rhône from Lyons to Avignon, one perpetual deluge – so that we were reduced to a hot crowded cabin on board a daily Steamboat. This was the climax; but in spite of all, the journey has been a happy one and I can never repent it.' There were also moral advantages in the experience: 'Nothing could have been better for Gerardine; if it had been arranged on purpose as a perpetual

*Letter printed in *Anna Jameson, Letters and Friendships* (1812–1860), edited by Mrs Steuart Erskine (Fisher Unwin, 1915).

lesson, it could not have been more effective and she has been really very good and very efficient *considering*.' At Avignon Mrs Browning was too ill to look at the town. She lay on her bed in the Hôtel de l'Europe listening to her companions' descriptions of the Palace of the Popes. She did succeed in accompanying them to the Fontaine de Vaucluse ('E.B. got through it very well'), but after two days in Avignon they decided to go on and catch the steamboat for Genoa at Marseilles. All the same, Avignon was a change from Wimpole Street, for as Mrs Jameson rapturously exclaimed in another letter from that town: 'We are in the *South* here, olive trees, figs, vines at every step.' Even the studious Anna Jameson was not immune to the overwhelming excitement of entering Provence.

VII

But not all of Anna Jameson's literary compatriots and contemporaries found the countryside of Avignon exciting and irresistible. Lady Blessington, settled for three winter months at the Hôtel de l'Europe with her husband and Count d'Orsay on their way to Italy in 1822, judged the splendid plains of Mistral featureless. 'Rode a considerable distance today,' she noted in her journal, 'but the country round Avignon is for the most part so flat and uninteresting, as to offer little temptation to explore it.' It was not until her party moved slowly southwards through Aix to Toulon in late February that the olive trees seemed to her 'larger and less sombre', the vegetation of a 'brilliant verdure', and the Provençal climate 'genial'.

In spite of a certain unconventionality in the arrangement of her personal life, Marguerite Blessington was in fact a woman of highly conventional tastes and mind. She shared her contemporaries' admiration for torrents, mountains and gorges – the valley of the Gardon, for example, she visited with rapture. She liked to muse about her letter-writing on the site of the vanished Château de Grignan, or to 'recline' beside the fountain of Petrarch at Vaucluse. She sometimes startled 'the dowagers and ancient spinsters of Avignon' by some 'feat' like riding her horse, Mameluke, over the Rhône bridge to the fortress of Villeneuve. But on the whole her journal, which Colburn published as *An Idler in Italy* in 1839, is filled with desultory, often banal, reflections on such subjects as the contrast between French and English ideas of conversation, or the fickleness of French women in love. Here and there are sharp or interesting comments – as when, for instance, she remarks that the wind in Avignon makes everyone you meet 'look like a gorgon'; 'curls are blown into straight and lanky locks; bonnets are twisted into most uncouth shapes'. Deciding, for some reason, that the people of southern France were 'more liable to diseases of the eye than those of any other part', she was astonished to observe that the inhabitants of Avignon all used umbrellas 'of a deep rose colour,' for she thought that this shade 'must be very injurious to the sight . . . On a wet day,' she adds, 'the streets resemble vast beds of damask roses put in motion, and has a fantastic and pretty effect.' Yet all the same, Lady Blessington had merits as a traveller which put most of us to shame. She voyaged not with pleasure only, but with learning.

'It is strange,' she tells us in one of the numerous sentences of the *Idler* which end with an exclamation mark, 'how soon the mind turns with new interest to pursuits that had previously engaged little of its thoughts!' After a passage on the 'mobility of the Intellect' as 'one of the manifold proofs of the wisdom and mercy of the Creator', the authoress explains that she has long formed the habit, while travelling, of preparing herself by a course of diligent reading for the sights that she is going to see. In the upholstered interior of her swaying travelling-carriage Lady Blessington would sit holding a Pliny or a 'Titus Livy' open on her lap. 'Evenings at a comfortless inn' would be spent comparing a theory of Pontanus with some statement by Peiresc. She would dip into Mandajors or Spon to see whether these authorities agreed with Guibs and Maffei on some controversial Roman date. Should a name be read Boduacus, Bituitus, or Betultus? She would pore over the life-work of the Baron de la Bastie or of her Avignon acquaintance, the Abbé Letbert, in an earnest effort to decide in which Emperor's honour was erected the triumphal arch 'well placed on a plain a few hundred paces in front of the town' of Orange in the Vaucluse. And when the carriages had actually rolled into Orange, she would step down, and, leaning on her husband's arm, discuss with him the vital question of whether the female figure resting her head on her hand upon the south front of the arch really represented the city of Massilia or was just another personification of Martha, the ubiquitous Syrian sibyl, who had attended Marius on his victorious campaigns.

The little country town of Orange, under Augustus a rich Roman colony, which later, by a series of uninteresting political irrelevancies, gave its name to the Dutch royal house, one King of England, a great river and a small state in Africa, and an Irish political party, has long been celebrated for the two major Roman monuments which it contains. The arch, which has puzzled not only Lady Blessington but generations of archaeologists and historians as well, stands somewhat bleakly outside the town. Rated the third finest Roman arch in Europe, it has suffered on the one hand from the wind, which has almost effaced the sculptures of its northern face, on the other from nineteenth-century restoration, but it survives as an elaborate, imposing structure, pierced by a large central and two smaller arches, and richly decorated with maritime and armorial bas-reliefs. Yet though unquestionably impressive it is less beautiful and so less moving than some of the smaller triumphal arches surviving in Provence. Apart from that at Saint-Rémy, which I shall later describe, there are two other of these trophies in the vicinity of Avignon which it is easy to overlook. One is the small arch in the dusty, melon-growing town of Cavaillon, the second is the exquisite arch at Carpentras, a place which also contains an important library, a magnificent Hôtel-Dieu completed in 1760, and a fine episcopal palace, designed by the seventeenth-century architect François de la Valfenière. It is in the sheltered courtyard of this bishop's palace, now used as a Palais de Justice, that the triumphal arch of Carpentras has most sensibly been placed. This arch, which has a single opening and has lost the whole of its pediment, is contemporaneous with that at Orange, though it is considerably less ornate. The sculptures in relief on two sides show barbarian captives clothed in animal skins and chained to trophies for some Roman triumph. The quality of these sculptures, the quiet and elegant position of the arch and a fig tree which grows beside it, and presses against the brownish-yellow stone leaf-fronds as green and delicate as those we see in the background of some of Holbein's English portraits, combine to make this arch rival and even, in my opinion, surpass the more notable example at Orange.

In Lady Blessington's day the Roman theatre of Orange, now carefully uncovered and preserved, was used partly as a criminal prison, and partly as the town refuse-dump. It also housed, in its dim inner passages, the many beggars who accosted strangers in the town. 'Here, where the comedies of Plautus and of Terence were enacted, we behold only the most disgusting details of poverty and uncleanliness,' Lady Blessington could not resist remarking, 'and where sat the proud and warlike Roman leaders, troops of squalid children and half-starved dogs disport.' But no amount of squalor could deter her from penetrating into the inmost passages of the theatre, and following a skeletal 'crone' who, with a blinking oil-lamp, conducted the rich English party round. Today you can wander at will about the carefully kept remains of this theatre and clamber up and down its gigantic semicircle of stone seats; but to those who, like myself, find the tremendous overpowering, the theatre of Orange will not be their happiest memory of a summer in Provence. There is something deeply intimidating in the size of such Roman ruins, and in the knowledge that they represent but a tithe of the original buildings – there were vast gymnasia next the Orange theatre, for instance, of which little now remains. The very size of the great blocks of Gallo-Roman masonry, hewn by a giant's hand, has something formidable about it, even when only a few stones remain standing, as in the ruins of that epoch at Senlis on the Oise. To come unwarned upon the colossal wall of masonry of the theatre at Orange, or to see for the first time the lofty galleries and gaping eye-sockets of the arena at Nîmes, is something of a shock. In towns, where one cannot help contrasting these leviathans with the miniature-looking houses in which the townspeople eat and live, the effect is alarming. But, isolated in the country as the Roman antiquities at Saint-Rémy-de-Provence are isolated, these remnants of an ancient civilization seem approachable. They become a part of the Provençal landscape, a natural phenomenon like the foothills of the Alpilles. This is true, above all, of that most superb of the Roman monuments within reach of Avignon, the aqueduct at the Pont du Gard.

CHAPTER THREE

I

'YOU WON'T BE ABLE TO STAND it here today,' said the old naturalist at the Hôtel du Pont du Gard. 'Let me recommend a walk in the vicinity.'

It was the morning of the annual spring *corrida* in Nîmes arena. Motor-cars, omnibuses, wooden booths and lemonade stalls, gipsy caravans, ranges for pigeon-shooting and tables for roulette had, since dawn, been turning the solemn, savage valley of the Gardon into a small inferno of vulgarity and noise. The old naturalist was English. He was a gentle and erudite person wearing shorts, pince-nez, and a high-domed straw topee, and he carried an ivory cane. He told me at breakfast that he had been to the Pont du Gard each May for the last twenty-five years, and I was not surprised. He came there, he explained, to watch a pair of white heron which nested near the bridge and flew above the water on bright days. Later in the month he would go southwards into the Crau and the Camargue, to look at the birds down there. The regularity of these visits, inter-rupted only by the war, seemed to me entirely comprehensible, for it was my own fourth journey in Provence, and I had already realized that I could never again let a year go by without travelling there for a few weeks at the least. Provence is a taste or more correctly a passion which once contracted cannot be cured. A nostalgia for it creeps over you each early springtime: you may feel it in London or in Paris, in the trim, tame fields of Wiltshire or in the white wooden houses of the Norwegian fjords. I was glad to meet a fellow-victim of this passion, and only too ready to take his advice and spend the morning walking away from the river Gardon towards Uzès and the hamlet of Vers.

Following his directions, we crossed the bridge which the Estates of Languedoc hitched on to one side of the viaduct in the eighteenth century, and scrambled up a sandy bank between small larch trees.

Soon we were walking across dry heathy country glowing with furze bushes in full flower, the air smelling strongly of thyme and wild rosemary, the ground dabbled with white and purple asters, small lilies and bee orchis. Swallowtail and white admiral butterflies flopped along in the sunshine, low down, on the level of our knees. When we emerged on to the high road to Vers we found it bordered on one hand by cherry orchards, on the other by long swerving fields of grass. Clusters of scarlet cherries were already gleaming through the shiny green leaves. Here and there along the road strange resolute clouds of dragonflies were hovering, apparently attracted by something in the trees. Their stiff bodies were a sharp metallic blue, and their transparent wings flashed and quivered in the sun.

Like many villages of Provence and of the western Rhône bank, Vers is perched up on a hillock. Like all of them, it is a place with few streets, few shops, a central square with plane trees, a small church, and a café. Hot and thirsty, we made straight for the café. At the back of it was a lofty saloon, with seedy brownish walls and iron tables, and a dais on which the instruments of a jazz band were loosely stacked. The only people in this room were three youths who lolled against the wall opposite the windows, drinking *pastis*. The youngest of them, a flushed fair boy of sixteen, wearing a thick tweed Sunday suit, had already drunk too much.

On the way to Vers we had passed, and listlessly examined, some arches of Roman masonry near a vineyard, and called locally Les Croisades. The naturalist had told us to look out for them, though after the Pont du Gard they seemed of very minor appeal. Yet their unexpected presence near the vineyard is characteristic of the whole countryside. The chief marks of the Roman colonization of the Midi are naturally found in the towns and cities of the Aurelian Way and of the Rhône banks – cities which, once pompous and luxurious, now strike us chiefly as sad, intimate and old. But all along the southern Rhône, and all across Provence, stand isolated vestiges of Rome. They range in scale and importance from the great viaduct behind us, or the single-span bridge over the Ouvèze at Vaison, to some broken monument, some piece of funeral pyramid or stump of ancient style in a field, some fragment of entablature or temple frieze built into the rough walls of a medieval farmhouse or stone stable.

Bits of these classical debris were collected in the last century and housed, together with excavated statues and unearthed sarcophagi, in *musées lapidaires* like those of the rococo chapel of the Lycée at Avignon, and in the church of Sainte-Anne at Arles. Others, left where they lay, continued to be the subjects of local folk-legends and of the ardent speculations of provincial antiquaries. These relics, together with the Latin derivations of many place-names, and such a fact as that one-fourth of the men of the country are still christened Marius after the victorious general who defeated the barbarians near Aix in 102 BC, give continuity and actuality to the Roman traditions of Provence.

Some tracts of France are still as wild and as resolutely un-inhabitable as the larger part of the North American continent. Provence is not amongst them, for at each step you realize that this rich countryside has been lived in and lived over for many centuries. Up in the hillside vineyards, down amongst the groves of twisted olive trees, you can smell antiquity. It seems present in the apple orchards round the town of Arles, in the resinous forests on the mountains west of Aix, and on the shores of maritime Provence along which the cumbrous Roman galleys would move from port to port, and where the pale and sweet mimosa flowers in lemon cataracts in early spring. This sense of Latin humanity, and of generations of individual human fates ripening and rotting like plums in the hot sun, gives you, as well, the strange sensation of never being totally alone. Even the deserted regions of High Provence seem drenched in human living. You can never forget that Provence, in the words of one of its most devoted historians, M. Berenger-Féraud, '*a été habitée dès l'âge de pierre*'.

In 1885, Berenger-Féraud, a retired naval doctor resident at Toulon, published a book on Marius' victories over the barbarians in the countryside of Mont Sainte-Victoire. Five years later he followed it up with a more diffuse and less instructive work: *Les Provençaux à travers les ages*. In both these books, the doctor used the term 'Provence' in the exclusive sense already current, and which remains legal and habitual through France today. He defined Provence, with its five departments, in the bleak and simple terms of a school geography – a territory of south-eastern France, bounded on the north by the old province of the Dauphiné, on the west by the flat lands of the Languedoc, on the east by the mountains of Piedmont, and on the south by the Mediterranean Sea. Within this irregular quadrilateral lie several contrasting varieties of landscape, yet all are variations upon a single theme. The whole area of Provence from the Maritime Alps to the Rhône, from the Dauphiné to the sea, is made homogeneous by the universal culture of the olive and the vine, by the language, traditions, ideas and physique of the people who inhabit it, and by the unmistakable stamp of a great classical civilization which Rome has left upon this country like the deeply cut impression of an imperial seal. Though technically in the Languedoc, Nîmes and the Pont du Gard belong by cultural tradition to Provence.

II

I was never at the Pont du Gard till 1949. That provincial suspicion which makes one distrust too-famous sights, that vanity which urges one to try to discover new or unknown places for oneself, had deterred me, as well as a pronounced distaste for the city of Nîmes. This spring of 1949 I and a companion were revisiting Provence by bus, a disastrous enterprise given the inconvenience of the buses and the arbitrary nature of their timetables. If you cannot take a car, it would be better to travel through Provence by bicycle or on foot, than by bus, for you would see the country properly and you would be more free. A bicyclist to whom I spoke one morning in the auditorium of the theatre at Orange (there is something so awe-inspiring, so inhuman about these greatest Roman monuments that you turn eagerly to any stranger for a word) told me he was going on later that day to the Pont du Gard. I had meant to do the same, but after an unhelpful conversation with the Syndicat d'Initiative at Orange my determination had wilted away. Hearing that someone intended to bicycle that considerable distance in the heat, I was ashamed. I decided to take the risk of finding a corresponding bus at Avignon for Remoulins, the bus-stop for the Pont du Gard. In a long experience of crowded and dirty French buses, I have never seen one so crushingly overloaded as that which we caught outside the ramparts that evening about six o'clock. We almost fell out of the bus at

Remoulins, which proved to be a huddle of three or four houses and some old women on a road. The bus lurched off, leaving us, our small handcase, and a bamboo rod on the tarmac in the evening light. We had been told that we should have to walk to the viaduct, and for a moment we did not know which way to go. Then, glancing over my shoulder, I saw suddenly that we were already in the presence of the Pont du Gard, which looked still and very yellow between the black foliage of trees in the setting sun. The viaduct was half a mile away, and by some optical trick due perhaps to the perfection of its architectural proportions, it appeared far smaller than I anticipated, almost miniature. It had, too (and this it retains on closer acquaintance), a quality of inevitability about it, as though it had grown there and had not been built: 'The Pont du Gard seems, more than anything else, the completion of a landscape that had been left unfinished by mistake.'*

Tobias Smollett, who visited the Pont du Gard in the autumn of 1763, has written that from the first distant view of the monument, until he came near enough to see it perfectly, he 'felt the strongest emotions of impatience' he had ever known. He was travelling by the slow, sure method of a mule-carriage, and when he caught sight of the viaduct he forced his driver to put the mules at full gallop for fear darkness would have fallen before he reached the place. The viaduct impressed him deeply – 'a piece of architecture so unaffectedly elegant, so simple and majestic, that I will defy the most phlegmatic and stupid spectator to behold it without admiration'. Exactly one hundred years later Charles Kingsley scribbled in an emotional letter to his wife that his first impression of the Pont du Gard 'was one of simple fear'.

Built in the reign of Augustus of biscuit-yellow blocks of un-cemented stone, the Pont du Gard spreads across its valley like some giant and branching oriental tree. The vast foundation arches in the river-bed are six in number. These support a wider tier of eleven lower arches, which in their turn carry a row of thirty-five others smaller still. This topmost line is capped by the flagged and covered channel, five feet deep, through which the water flowed from Uzès to Nîmes. The slow majestic beauty of the Pont du Gard is due to a

*Shrines and Cities of France and Italy, by Evelyn Underhill (Longmans, Green, 1949).

coincidence of many factors – its actual scale and architectural perfection, the radiant colour of its ancient stones, its total isolation in this wild valley so that we see it as relative only to clear water and to trees. Of essential importance, too, is the fine romantic landscape of the Gardon valley, a tumbling river with trout pools, cascades and sandy banks and reaches, shut in by steep walls of feathery trees, a southern version of the river Tees near Rokeby. That spring evening the whole high monument, the river water and the crowding trees seemed to shimmer in the late sunlight. Prosper Mérimée (who saw it during his 1835 journey on a day of storm, and described it as illuminated by a single shaft of sunlight falling from a dark and gloomy sky, the Gardon swollen, roaring and '*couleur de café*') was sufficient of a Romantic to realize how much Nature in this case has aided Art: '*Le site sauvage*,' he wrote, '*la solitude complète du lieu, le bruit du torrent, ajoutaient une poésie sublime à l'architecture imposante qui s'offrait à mes yeux*.' The comments of different generations upon a single sight are curiously revealing. What could be further from Mérimée's Romantic viewpoint than Smollet's final comment on this scene: 'If I lived at Nismes or Avignon . . . I should take pleasure in forming parties to come hither, in summer, to dine under one of the arches of the Pont du Gard, on a cold collation.'

III

We crossed the eighteenth-century bridge beneath the arches, pausing to peer down into the river in which some girls were swimming vaguely in the waning heat. Across the river, and well away from the viaduct, stands the old Hôtel du Pont du Gard, a comfortable building with a garden, a dining-room constructed like a Swiss châlet and shut in by glass, and a garage in a prehistoric cave. This hotel has lately acquired a rival, in the shape of a stone mill-house far down the river on the other bank. In certain famous places of the Midi there is now a tendency to replace, or supplement, the old hotels by expensive modern ones decorated in a self-consciously Provençal style. These are places to avoid.

After an excellent meal we walked along the road to the viaduct, which shone above us in the moonlight. Climbing the little twisting path that leads up the cliff face, through tangled thorn and wild fruit bushes, we emerged on the summit. At our feet the viaduct led straight across the river. We began to walk along the top. The first steps gave one a feeling of vertigo, for in places the ledge narrows, and looking down a hundred feet into the river water, where the moon's reflection lies like a submerged disc, gives you a suicidal impulse to jump off. Kingsley, who walked the length of the viaduct in daylight shortly after it had been repaired by order of Napoleon III, said that no one who felt giddy should attempt it, but that he of course did not mind.

Far below in the green water, you could see trout darting in the moonlight. Standing in the centre of the viaduct, we looked out across the tree-tops towards the plain of Avignon and the valley of the Rhône. In that light spring night you sensed Provence stretching out before you, eastwards to the Maritime Alps, southwards to the Mediterranean Sea.

CHAPTER FOUR

I

ONE GLIMPSE OF THE GREAT STRUCTURE of the Pont du Gard –
better still, a day or two passed in its company – leaves you with a
conception of the colonizing power of Rome which nothing will
impair. And as you cross the river Rhône, leaving the Languedoc for
Provence itself, each town and village seems to offer you some dusty
testimony to the splendour of late Roman civilization in southern
Gaul, making you more than ever conscious of the strong classical
roots of Provençal culture. Many of these Roman relics are military
and triumphal in their form and nature; and to gain an idea of the
sophistication of Graeco-Roman civil life as it was lived beside the
salt lagoons into which the river Rhône then flowed, you must go to
the ancient seaport of Arles, once a prosperous Roman colony of one
hundred thousand inhabitants, later the capital of Gaul, and now a
decayed, bustling Provençal township where less than twenty thousand persons live: '*Arles*' wrote Stendhal in 1837, '*est un trou où le
voyageur ne va que pour ses admirables antiquités.*'

In Arles you must, obviously enough, visit the arena, at once
larger, less sinister and more authentic than that of Nîmes. You
must linger in the ruins of the antique Greek theatre, with its two
elegant columns of African and Carrara marbles upright in the still,
soft air. You must wander in the Alyscamps, between the empty
stone sarcophagi shaded by cypress trees. But you must also (and
this less picturesque task may need more determination) look
carefully at the contents of the Musée Lapidaire in the desecrated
church of Sainte-Anne on the Place de la République. In this museum
is assembled a quantity of pagan sarcophagi, some important
fragments of sculpture, the bruised head from a colossal statue of
the Emperor Augustus, a very beautiful bust of an unidentified
Empress, a fine Roman altar with bas-reliefs, and some pieces of
mosaic floor – all objects disinterred within the city at one epoch or

another, and not deemed sufficiently notable to be sent – like the Vénus d'Arles discovered in 1651, or the porphyry pillars from the theatre which were shipwrecked in the Rhône in the reign of Charles IX – to embellish Versailles or the Louvre. Mutilated and disparate though they be, the contents of this small museum make a grand cumulative effect. Small and broken works of art, they give you a sense of intimacy you cannot derive from the aqueducts, amphitheatres or wind-scrubbed triumphal arches of Provence. This museum was termed by Henry James 'the most Roman thing I know of, out of Rome'.*

Since the object of this book is to provide a commentary upon certain aspects of Provence, and not to examine its monuments chronologically, I do not propose to club the Roman relics of Provence together in one chapter, but to notice them as they occur.† But if one is to get best value out of places visited, some skeletal knowledge of their history is necessary, and this seems particularly true of Roman places, for classical history, last read at school, is for most people a subject indistinct and blurred. Whatever aesthetic or romantic pleasure one may experience on gazing at the Pont du Gard or on standing in early morning before the formidable walls of the theatre at Orange, one wishes to know something of the reason for the existence of these giant structures: faced with the lonely biscuit-coloured arches of Orange or Carpentras or Saint-Rémy or Cavaillon, one does wonder what they commemorate, and why. Too often the answers are uncertain: the famous mausoleum upon the Plateau des Antiques at Saint-Rémy has been accounted among other things a monument to Caius Marius to commemorate his victory at Pourrières, a monument to the young grandsons of Augustus Caesar and the tomb of a rich Christian family of Glanum of the second century. To the uninstructed traveller these disputes among experts are bewildering; yet, while it is not always possible to

*Henry James visited Arles in 1870 and again in 1882. On this latter occasion he included an account of the town in the series of travel articles he was then writing for *Harper's Magazine* and which he published in book form in 1885 as *A Little Tour in France*. A new edition of the *Little Tour* appeared in 1949.

†A short, intelligent and readable study of these monuments is to be found in the first volume of Sir Theodore Andrea Cook's admirable *Old Provence* (Rivingtons, 1905).

name the builder or define the purpose of some specific Roman monument, it is not at all so difficult to ascertain its period, and to keep the dates of the Roman occupation of Provence within one's head. Sightseeing is by no means the only object of a journey, but it is as unintelligent as it is lazy not to equip ourselves to understand the sights we see.

Like the history of every other country, the early history of Provence is one of invasions and of war. Vineyards which now lie calm beneath the evening sky have been the scenes of vast and bloody contests, and half the fields we see are battlefields. Plutarch records that one hundred thousand barbarians were slain in the two battles near Aix-en-Provence in which Marius defeated them in 102 BC, while Livy and other historians have put the dead on these occasions at twice that figure. Florus declares that the waters of the tranquil river Arc ran scarlet with blood after this battle, while Plutarch further describes how for generations the people of Marseilles would make the fences round their vineyards from barbarians' whitened bones.

The first occupation of Provence, by Greeks from the island of Rhodes, took place in the eighth century before Christ; it was followed two hundred years later by the arrival of other Greeks from Phocaea, and by a long period in which the Greek citizens of Massalia (Marseilles) and the Rhône delta fought a series of successful wars against the people of Carthage and Etruria. But in 154 BC, the Massaliotes appealed to Rome for aid against the Celts; within the next fifty years the Romans had taken over southern Gaul, and established the province of Gallia Narbonensis. The pacification of this territory was conducted in the usual Roman manner – a long coastal road was built, strong military posts were founded (Aquae Sextiae, the largest, in 122 BC), and finally in 118 BC a colony of Roman citizens was established at Narbo Martius. No sooner had this civilizing process got under way, than an unexpected danger appeared from the north, in the grim, ferocious shape of the barbarian hordes, the Cimbri and the Teutones, who swept like wolves across Europe, and inflicted a series of violent defeats upon the Roman armies, the most severe being that at Orange in the autumn of 105. Fortunately unaware of their own strength, the barbarians turned aside to ravage Spain, thus giving the Romans three years' grace to prepare the defence of southern Gaul and to block the open road to Italy. In 102 BC they attacked the reorganized Roman army which Marius had assembled on carefully chosen ground near Aix: in two successive battles the barbarians were annihilated. The sack of the antique world was deferred four centuries.

These two battles, one beside the river Arc to the south-west of Aix, its sequel near the hilltop village of Pourrières in the great plain farther eastward, are still commemorated each April in Provence, for the Fête de la Sainte-Victoire, held annually in such hamlets of the area as Trets, Perthuis and Vauvenargues, and long since transformed into a Christian festival, is believed to originate in the great nocturnal celebration which Marius and his soldiers staged in honour of their victory. It has been estimated that more than one-fourth of the male population of Provence are christened Marius, while a local superstition of the Aix countryside attributes to the ruthless employment of barbarian prisoners as quarry-slaves the unhappy haunted atmosphere of the hillside forests and mountain clefts of the locality outside Aix from which the stones of the city were hewn, and which is now occupied by the artificial lake of the Barrage Zola and the Petite Mer. A low heap of stones, protected by a wire fence but otherwise untidy and neglected, lying in a field beside the Aix–Brignoles road, is believed to be all that is left of a trophy erected by Marius after the battle. Strewn amongst the long dry grasses of the field, these stones may be seen a few yards from the bridge of la Petite-Pougière on the by-road to Pourrières. They show signs of having been chiselled, but are not worth making a detour to see. The village of Pourrières is a strangely silent hamlet, standing on a hillock in the plain on which this momentous battle was fought out.

From 58 BC to 51 BC, Julius Caesar conquered most of Gaul: in 49 BC Trebonius completed this conquest by the capture of Massalia, and this great port and city was afterwards included in the careful organization of Provence under Augustus Caesar. This organization, on the customary pattern of a series of cities and strong-points in a country otherwise uninhabited, survived until the fall of the Roman Empire, when Arles, for long the chief town of the province, and, after the capture of Trèves by the barbarians in AD 418, the capital city of Gaul, was conquered by the Visigothic king, Euric I, and the country south of the Durance fell under Visigothic rule. From that time on, the Roman monuments and buildings of the cities of Provence ceased to be respected. Many of them were lost and damaged in sieges and sacks, or were used as building material for the Christian churches and the castles which later centuries erected in Provence. During the Middle Ages certain Roman cities, such as Aix, retained their old consequence, or, like papal Avignon, acquired a new one. Others, like Arles, were put to sack, and gradually shrank in size as in importance. The arena of Arles was fortified and sheltered two hundred little huts and houses (only cleared away in the early nineteenth century), while the Greek theatre became the site of a monastery. Still other Roman cities of Provence have disappeared entirely beneath the crimson soil, abandoned when their inhabitants fled to take refuge, as at Vaison, on a rock and to make a new town there, or moved a few kilometres to a more convenient site, as the citizens of Glanum seem to have done when they founded Saint-Rémy. The theatre at Vaison has only recently emerged once more from its hillside; Glanum, now revealed by excavation, contains the only Grecian houses known in France.

To all but trained archaeologists the shallow trough-like foundations of Glanum, exposed beside the road from Saint-Rémy to Les Baux, are not inspiring; but opposite them stand two of the noblest monuments of Roman Provence – the elaborate triumphal arch erected by Julius Caesar to commemorate the taking of Marseilles, and the pyramidal monument, miscalled the 'mausoleum', with its enigmatic bas-reliefs, and its two anonymous male figures in togas side by side beneath the pillared cupola which crowns the whole. These two monuments, and the turfy Plateau des Antiques on which they stand, are in themselves well worth a journey to Provence to see.

II

By far the most enticing town in all this western region of Provence, Saint-Rémy is built upon a slight knoll, and from its higher ground presides benignly over an idyllic plain of vine plants and olive trees, growing in fields protected from the wind by screens of cypresses.

These black cypress screens, first seen near Avignon as one enters Provence from the west have nothing in common with the solitary ornamental cypress trees of Tuscany: utilitarian in their purpose, they are only accidentally elegant; brittle-looking, almost oriental, they are in fact a lithe and practical defence against the howling of the mistral, for they are flexible but tough, and set so closely that their branches knit together. Just as its vineyards, orchards and olive groves are protected from the wind by these screens, so is the town of Saint-Rémy itself protected from the mistral by the neighbouring range of the lilac-grey Alpilles, those wild and miniature mountains to whose topmost crest the desolate fortress village of Lex Baux clings like an eyrie.

Saint-Rémy, a place whose citizens are almost all involved in nursery gardening – for the production of flower seeds, not, as at Grasse, for the manufacture of scent – is a graceful, pastoral town, in aspect as in atmosphere a light contrast to the mournful streets of Arles, paved with the fragments of antiquity, and to the sordid remnants of the medieval city of Les Baux, as dismal and pot-holed as they are forbidding. Yet Saint-Rémy is often regarded by foreigners merely as the place you stop at when you visit Les Baux, or wish to examine what Augustus Hare with strange hyperbole describes as 'the magnificent ruins' of Glanum Livii, two kilometres beyond the town upon the Maussanne road. In reality, Saint-Rémy is a place to stay in for its own sake, as Gertrude Stein wisely perceived when she spent the year 1922 in the hotel there, writing *Capital Capitals, Saints and Singing*, and *Lend a Hand or Four Religions*. The birthplace of the prophet Nostradamus, as well as of the nineteenth-century Provençal poet and founder of the Félibrige movement, Joseph Roumanille, whose father was a gardener there, Saint-Rémy can also claim the honour of having been painted by van Gogh during the one year May 1889 to May 1890 when he was a patient at the asylum of Saint-Paul-du-Mausolée, and of being the place in which Gounod composed, and first played, his opera based on Mistral's *Mireille*. The people of Saint-Rémy are not unaware of these connections with a greater world: a fountain with the enigmatic bearded head of Nostradamus carved upon it stands against the wall of a narrow street corner in the old town, a plaque on the Hôtel de la Ville Verte commemorates Gounod's sojourn there while composing his opera; the nuns of the tranquil lunatic asylum near the Plateau des Antiques keep empty for exhibition the bare, square room in which Vincent van Gogh was bolted up. But apart from any such associations, Saint-Rémy has signal merits and beauties of its own. In springtime it takes on the rich light colour, and the serene atmosphere, of some little Tuscan town.

In size and shape, Saint-Rémy seems distinctly more manageable than some of the other rather straggling, attenuated towns of Provence. A certain superficial order seems imposed upon it – on the ground-plan in the guide at least – by a circular boulevard which encompasses the old town, confining it with all the safety of a wall, and keeping any modern developments such as garages well away. The great white classical church of Saint-Martin, a grandiose, unsuitable construction of the reign of Charles X, and preserving of its medieval predecessor only the belfry built by Pope John XII, is the first thing you notice about Saint-Rémy. Standing at the top of a flight of steps, which has become the rendezvous for the buses to Avignon and Arles, the church surveys the wide Place de la République, where the booths and merry-go-rounds are pitched each September for the town's three-day fête. But once you penetrate inside the old town itself, this sense of spaciousness proves an illusion, and a feeling of friendly claustrophobia prevails. Like the maps of many Latin towns, the ground-plan of Saint-Rémy in the *Guide Bleu* gives quite a false impression of the streets' importance, and of the town's size: one grandly named street after another turns out to be a winding lane. In the centre of Saint-Rémy is an oblong *place*, with plane trees and shops. One side of it is occupied by an arcaded building of the seventeenth century, once a convent but now the Mairie. This building with its arcades across the pavement might be a segment of some street in Mantua, and is particularly lovely seen by moonlight in the spring.

The museum of Saint-Rémy, an affair of bits of pottery from Glanum Livii, and bread-cupboards from Provençal *mas*, is housed in the nicest building of the town, the former hôtel of the family of Mistral de Montdragon (ancestors of the poet Frédéric Mistral), and popularly miscalled La Maison de Nostradamus. The Hôtel de Mistral de Montdragon is a long, dignified three-storeyed building, which would in Italy rank as a *palazzo*. Provincial, but not entirely unsophisticated, it has flat pilasters between the six windows of its upper storey, a cornice decorated with stone balls, and a gutter with griffin heads at either end. The hotel is situated on the tiny Place Favier, more like a room than an open space, and with a very large fountain in the centre of it, and some very small plane trees all around. The houses along the other sides of the Place Favier are washed yellow or pink. They have wooden shutters painted pale emerald green, and on their window-ledges and by their doorways squat cacti in pots of a chrome yellow so sharp and brilliant that one can't help being reminded of van Gogh. The water in the fountain makes a curious heavy gulping noise – not a splash or a gurgle – as one sits beside it, facing the Hôtel Mistral: for this small deserted square is a charming place to sit and think in Saint-Rémy, indeed the best place that I found except for the cold marble sarcophagi ranged as seats beneath the stone-pines round the Roman monuments at Glanum, or the unkempt garden of the tinny Café Robinson beside those ruins. An intelligent English lady of the last century, Madame James Darmesteter, who was brought to Saint-Rémy by Mistral and his wife in April 1892, and found there 'a waft of Italy', writing of the town for *The Contemporary Review*,* prettily describes its outlying streets as 'avenues of great zebra-trunked, century-old plane trees, garlanded in April with quaint little hanging balls, or else of wych-elms, gay with pinkish-buff blossoms, and yet so gnarled and hollow that they might almost be those famous elms which Sully planted about the towns of France'. 'We fell in love,' writes Madame Darmesteter, 'with Saint-Rémy.'

III

Like many Provençal towns, Saint-Rémy has shrunk from its former size, and the town limits are now filled out by orchards, hay-fields, and those flower gardens which give the place its old local designation, La Ville Verte. In the spring these gardens, which you pass on any road leading out of Saint-Rémy, but most of all perhaps upon

*Madame Darmesteter's article is to be found in volume 62 of *The Contemporary Review* (1892), p. 647.

the road to the Plateau des Antiques and Glanum, are filled with rambling roses, dark red and bright red, and with those other 'summer flowers' which in Provence bloom four months earlier than they do in England. Staying one April at the Hôtel de la Ville Verte, where Gounod wrote *Mireille*, and which is kept by a family of considerable charm, I would often walk the short distance from the town to the Plateau des Antiques, along an uphill road flanked by rose gardens and silver olive trees. On the way one passes an ugly bust of Gounod on a pedestal, and a touching little fifteenth-century chapel, enlarged in the sixteen-fifties, and dedicated to Our Lady of Pity. The chapel is exceedingly simple, with a fine wooden altar rail and a gentle smiling figure of the Virgin in white marble. Another half-mile's walk delivers one to the Plateau des Antiques.

The two monuments of this plateau – the 'mausoleum' and the triumphal arch – must once have dominated some major public quarter of the city of Glanum Livii, thronged by the Gaulish citizens of that not unimportant place. Today they stand alone. The turfy ground from which they rise is bright in spring with poppies, and planted with stone-pines which slope at wind-blown angles. On April and May mornings the air is scented with lime flowers, and the monuments make long shadows on the grass, firm and architectural; while the stone-pines cast the crazy shadows of trees shaped by the wind. The stones of the triumphal arch and the 'mausoleum' are gold-coloured. Behind them, hardly a stone's-throw away, the first ashy crags of the Alpilles jut from the coarse grass. This outcrop of the range is riddled with caverns, old quarries, and the sites of rock-dwellings; footpaths ragged with honeysuckle lead in and out amongst the rocks, and you may take many tortuous routes to the summit of some small peak, to look down upon the monuments and the town of Saint-Rémy. The road to Maussanne and Les Baux winds mysteriously away round a corner in this rocky landscape, continuing on and up through a wasteland of crags that Robida* has aptly described as '*du Gustave Doré extraordinaire*', and which make one think that one is walking in the mountains on the moon.

*The fourth of the quarto volumes of *La Vieille France: texte, dessins et lithographies par A. Robida* is devoted to Provence. Published at the turn of the century, Robida's works are both useful and instructive (Paris, à la Librairie Illustrée, n.d.).

The setting of the town of Glanum Livii must have been one of the most dramatic in all Gaul.

The yellowish foundations of Glanum itself lie a little way beyond the two monuments, on the opposite side of the road. To the un-initiated a maze of meaningless trenches, these excavations clearly reveal to archaeologists the site of a forum, Roman baths, temples, and a Christian basilica, as well as many private houses and the only Greek dwellings yet unearthed in France. The town was sacked in AD 480; and Glanum, which originally came into being as a centre for the quarrying and hewing of stones needed in the expansion of Arelatum (Arles), must in its turn have become a quarry for the construction of the new town of Freta, today Saint-Rémy. If one has not a very vivid historical imagination it is impossible to connect these muddy remains, and the two splendid lonely monuments upon their tableland of sward, with a populous city, crowded with persons in togas going about their daily life. No series of repeated sessions on the sarcophagi, or watchful visits to the Café Robinson, can persuade one that this silent, magnificent plateau was once agog with civic life. So dead, or so impersonal, is the atmosphere in which these ruins are embalmed that even the lean curs of the Café Robinson – a raddled little restaurant selling postcards and *apéritifs* which lurks behind the stone-pines four hundred yards from the Plateau, its garden a tangle of unpruned roses – seem unreal as they lope in threatening packs towards some solitary tourist, in the perpetually disappointed hope of food.

The triumphal arch of Glanum, with its fine ornamented interior, its archivolt garlanded with stone leaves, fruit and flowers, ranked by Mérimée as equal to anything in the sculptured detail of the Gothic period, and the fine figures of captive prisoners in chains, is thought the earliest of all such buildings erected by the Romans outside the borders of Italy. The authorities generally agree that the arch must have been erected on Julius Caesar's orders shortly after 49 BC to commemorate the capture by Trebonius of the great port of Massalia (Marseilles). Sir Theodore Cook inclines to think the arch now stands higher than it did originally, and that the base has been too deeply excavated; while the author of *The Architecture of Provence and the Riviera* finds the opening of the arch too low. This divergence of opinion on the triumphal arch is nothing to the positive welter of conflicting theories to which its neighbour the pyramidal 'maus-oleum' has given rise.

The 'mausoleum' stands on a four-square base, ornamented with scenes in bas-relief, which have been variously interpreted to fit the various theories of the monument's date and purpose. Extremely difficult to see, they may indeed represent, as Mérimée first said they did, a hunting party, a fight of Amazons, the death of Patroclus, and a skirmish of cavalry. They fit equally with Sir Theodore Cook's theory of scenes from the triumphs of Caius Marius, in whose post-humous honour he believes the monument to have been raised. Again, the most recent theory that the scenes are connected with the career and deaths of Augustus's two grandsons, Caius and Lucius, who died in their youth, one in Syria, the other in Spain, seems very plausible, and would certainly explain the presence of two male figures in togas standing side by side within the pillared cupola which surmounts the monument. It is generally agreed that an inscription on the architrave of the north side, declaring it to be a memorial erected by three members of the Julian family to their parents, and proved by the evidence of spelling and form to be at least a century later than the monument itself, has no bearing on the original purpose of the building; these Julii would seem to have appropriated in the first or second century, and used as a private family tomb, an old public monument of Glanum. The ambiguity of this fine monument and the cloud of imprecision which sheathes its origins add to the sense of mystery created by the isolation of these antique ruins, solemn reminders of mortality, stranded upon the very boundaries of the eerie territory of Les Baux and the ravines of the Alpilles.

I may add that the Plateau des Antiques and the ruins of Glanum Livii are among several places in Provence that I should not re-commend imaginative persons to visit alone by the light of the moon.

IV

Standing for eighteen centuries in the silence of the foothills of the Alpilles, these noble monuments have naturally become the subjects of much local folklore in the district. The most widely believed legend, still current today, is of a golden goat that guards, deep in the earth beneath the pyramid of the Julii, a treasure of fantastic worth. The author of an excellent short modern account of the asylum of Saint-Rémy* has pointed out that the influence of this legend can even be traced in one of the prophecies of Nostradamus, who, born in a street in the ramparts of Saint-Rémy in 1503, must often have seen the monuments in his youth. The couplet, as intentionally obscure as all of Nostradamus's prophecies, runs:

> *De Pol Mausol dans Caverne caprine*
> *Cache et prins, extrait hors par la barbe.*

'*Caverne caprine*' is clearly a reference to the *cabro d'or*, or golden goat, of the old legend: 'Pol Mausol' is the church and asylum of Saint-Paul-du-Mausolée (also called Saint-Paul-de-Mausole), hidden behind a high wall at the end of an avenue of stone-pines some half-mile from the monuments at Glanum.

Saint-Paul-de-Mausole is a large twelfth-century church with a Louis Quinze façade, a twelfth-century cloister, and the buildings of a former monastery which have been used since 1605 as an asylum for the detention of the insane. Apparently founded in the tenth century, Saint-Paul had its great period four hundred years later as an archdiaconate to the cathedral church of Avignon. Repeated devastations of the town of Saint-Rémy during the wars of religion in the last third of the sixteenth century left Saint-Paul in a state of decay from which it was revived by the Observantine Brothers to whom the church and monastery were granted in 1605. A mendicant order, the Observantines converted the conventual buildings into an asylum in which, until the French Revolution, lunatic members of Provençal families and certain persons condemned by *lettres de cachet*, were kept. This institution and other Observantine activities, such as looking after the little chapel of Our Lady of Pity, and building a straight road from the town to the Plateau des Antiques, were so useful, that when the National Assembly decreed the closing of many religious houses in 1790, the town council of

Saint-Paul-de-Mausole à Saint-Remy-de-Provence: notes historiques et touristiques, by Dr Edgar Leroy. Published by the local Syndicat d'Initiative, this pamphlet may be purchased in the town.

Saint-Rémy petitioned for a reprieve in the case of the community of Saint-Paul-du-Mausolée. This petition failed, and the Observantines were forced to leave, taking their charges with them. In the spring of 1791, the church and buildings were sold. Unable to reorganize and reopen the asylum, the purchasers resold it sixteen years later to a certain Doctor Mercurin of Saint-Rémy, a man of many strange and some enlightened ideas about the treatment of dementia, one of them being a cure by music. From the reign of Napoleon I onwards, the asylum of Saint-Paul-du-Mausolée has continued to function as a state-owned institution, looked after until 1866 by the sisters of Saint-Vincent-de-Paul, and since then by those of Saint-Joseph d'Aubenas. But to us the paramount interest of Saint-Paul, and of its old luxuriant garden, must be the fact that here, from the spring of 1889 to the spring of 1890, Vincent van Gogh lived, painting some of his last and finest pictures, and writing to his brother and to his friend Émile Bernard those marvellous letters – vital, sensitive, modest and humane – which are without any equal in the literature of the European painting of the nineteenth century. Those acquainted with this correspondence will approach the blank wall of Saint-Paul-du-Mausolée – sheltered by stone-pines and pink chestnut trees, the whole wild landscape of the Alpilles unfurled on either hand – in a spirit of excitement tinged with awe.

In reply to a tug of the bell – sometimes several tugs of the bell – an aged porteress nun diligently unlocks the wicket door beside the big gate in the garden wall; you step through this little doorway into a garden as brilliant, lush and entangled as any in the islands of the Antilles. This efflorescence comes, of course, in springtime; for by midsummer the gardens of Provence are bare and bronzed, with hardly a flower upon a stalk. The long path down which the nun directs you is weed-grown, bordered by irises, and shaded by pines, lindens and chestnut trees; a stone urn with a stone garland round it exudes geraniums; everywhere there are tendrils of ivy and other creeping plants. Amongst the ground-ivy at the trees' roots pale periwinkles shine. With the high wall and the low door, the lofty ill-kept trees and the rush of flowers, it seems indeed the *Secret Garden* of the children's novel of Frances Hodgson Burnett.

The cloister, when you reach it, is also filled with flowers: oleander trees and three *néfliers du Japon* grow in the central square, with white geraniums in pots, and tall, thin rose trees carrying white roses in profusion. The cloister itself is small and fine. Its pillars, supporting capitals carved with whorled designs of leaves and little grotesque faces, are comparable in quality and motif to those of the far larger cloisters of the same date to be seen at Saint-Trophime in Arles, and at the desecrated abbey of Montmajour between Arles and Saint-Rémy. In the cloister of Saint-Paul there broods an atmosphere of extreme peace, even though the silence may at times be pierced by a distant cataract of laughter or a wailing cry which reminds one suddenly of the purpose of the place. But these cries come seldom: on one balmy morning in late April I remember that the only sound in church, cloister or garden was the dry rustling of a broom against the cloister paving, as a stout, full-skirted nun earnestly brushed the stones.

It is best to look first at the sun-filled cloister, with its cheerful pillar-heads and tumbling flowers, before plunging through an ivied doorway and down dank stairs into the corridor on which van Gogh's cell opens. The cell is square and plain, with two grey-painted doors – one giving access to the next room, one to the corridor – and a fairly large window with bars, giving on to a prospect of fields. Van Gogh (who several times in his letters makes the point that the Arles–Camargue country is like the Holland of Ruysdael and Hobbema, the chief difference being the sulphur-yellow 'of everything the sun lights on'), compared the view through this window to a picture by van Goyen: 'Through the iron-barred window,' he wrote, 'I see a square of corn in an enclosure, a perspective like van Goyen, above which I see in the morning the sun rising in his glory.' At the time van Gogh occupied it, the little room had a 'greenish-grey' wallpaper, and 'two curtains of sea-green with a design of very pale roses, brightened by slight touches of blood-red'. 'These curtains,' wrote the painter, 'probably the relics of some rich and ruined defunct, are very pretty in design. From the same source probably comes a very worn armchair, re-covered with an upholstery splashed like a Diaz or a Monticelli, with brown, red, rose, white, cream, black, forget-me-not blue and bottle-green.'* When van Gogh was in

*Letter to Theo of 25 May 1889, printed as letter No. 592 of *Further Letters of Vincent van Gogh to his Brother, 1886–1889* (Constable and Co., 1929).

the asylum, there were more than thirty rooms empty; one of these he was allowed to use as a studio. Much of his time in the long sane productive intervals between his fits, he spent painting in the garden or, when permitted, in the fields beyond the walls. In bad weather the patients, with nothing to amuse or occupy them, and no work to do, were herded together in a big common-room, which van Gogh has also painted. 'The room where we stay on wet days is like a third-class waiting-room in some dead-alive village,' he wrote to Theo, 'the more so as there are some distinguished lunatics who always wear a hat, spectacles, and cane, and travelling cloak, like at a bathing resort almost, and they represent the passengers.' 'What a pity one cannot shift this building here,' he wrote to his brother on another occasion. 'It would be splendid to hold an exhibition in, all the empty rooms, the great windows.' Judged objectively on his own evidence, the twelve months which van Gogh spent at Saint-Paul-du-Mausolée, then in the kindly incompetent care of a Monsieur Peyron, were not, in spite of his attacks and the depression his surroundings often caused him, months of such despair as was his earlier time at Arles, when crowds of hooligans, attracted by the incident of the severed ear, would clamour outside his yellow house, yelling 'Fou roux! Fou roux!' The propinquity, in the asylum, of so many unbalanced persons – the dirty and positively dangerous were segregated from the rest – and their kindness to each other, helped to exorcize his terror of his own mental attacks.

The most perceptive of contemporary writers on van Gogh* has observed that in spite of the 'long and varied list of mental diseases' produced since the painter's death to explain his case, no really convincing medical diagnosis has ever been pronounced. 'In his worst moments,' writes this critic, 'van Gogh's case may have amounted to temporary madness, though the most probable explanation of the facts seems to be that he was simply what is now called "manic depressive".' There are certainly no symptoms of derangement in the pictures that he painted either at Arles or at Saint-Paul-du-Mausolée: indeed the composition of many of them,

*Mr Douglas Lord, whose edition and translation of van Gogh's *Letters to Emil Bernard* (Crescent Press, 1938) is a model of scholarship and sanity.

most notably of his great painting of the asylum garden, must have required a sustained effort of the most clear-headed calculation and concentrated will we can conceive.

It is relevant to note that van Gogh himself inclined to attribute some part of his attacks to the effect of being in the south. When he at length determined that he must leave Saint-Rémy, he told his brother to explain to Monsieur Peyron that 'by a return to the north his illness will diminish, while by a more prolonged stay in the south, his condition would threaten to become more acute',* and it is in fact plausible to suppose that the intense emotional strain resulting from the impact of a Latin landscape and environment upon this northern genius may have brought to the surface that underlying 'form of psychic disturbance' which had driven him as a young man from art-dealing to preaching, and from preaching to painting. For van Gogh is above all a northern genius: 'I cannot manage to see the south like the good Italians,' he wrote to his brother from Saint-Rémy, '. . . on the contrary I see it more and more with a northerner's eyes!' Not being a Frenchman, he lacked the balance of a painter like Cézanne: he approached the Provençal world and its colours with unrestrained emotion, and as an outsider. 'Cézanne like Zola is so absolutely part of the countryside, and knows it so intimately, that you must make the same calculations in your head to arrive at the same tones,' he wrote in another letter.† He may have thought he made the same calculations, but he arrived neither at the same tones nor the same vision as Cézanne. This essentially northern or Teutonic aspect of van Gogh's genius was first adequately emphasized by Mr Douglas Lord, who claims him as 'the first painter ever to come so near a realization of southern conditions', and attributes this to his northern origin. Van Gogh may thus be regarded as the supreme, the pre-eminent interpreter of the landscape and people, the spirit and the atmosphere of Provence, in northern terms. For this reason an examination of his work is vital for any other northerner who wishes to understand Provence. For this reason too his letters from the south are of an interest and importance it is hard to overstate.

*Letter to his brother of May 1890, printed as No. 631 of the edition quoted above.
†Letter No 497, undated.

V

The incidents of Vincent van Gogh's two-year period in Provence have been dramatized by cheap biographers until the story of how he cut off one of his own ears and sent it in an envelope to an Arlesian girl is more widely known than anything else about him, and is treated as a subject of morbid interest by people who would never dream of looking at a painting. The facts of his sojourn in the Midi are simple, and easy to summarize. Suddenly deciding to leave Paris, where he had been working for two of the six years he had so far devoted to painting, van Gogh reached Arles in February 1888, some weeks before his thirty-fifth birthday. He settled in a room above the Restaurant Carrel – the *Night Café* of his famous picture – and in September of that year he moved to a small yellow house on the Place Lamartine, in which he had hired four rooms. Here, on 20 October, he welcomed Gauguin, come south at his invitation and with the idea that they should live and work together in Arles. Owing to Gauguin's odious disposition, this plan did not operate as well as van Gogh had expected, and after a few weeks of intense strain he had a species of fit, during which he hacked off an ear and sent it to a café girl as a present on Christmas Eve. He was admitted to the hospital at Arles, released, had a further attack, and was finally committed, at his own request, to Saint-Paul-du-Mausolée in May 1889. In June he began to paint the fields and olive groves outside the asylum walls. In July he visited Arles, and had another fit on his return; further visits to Arles produced the same result, and at length, determined that Saint-Paul and its superintendent could do him nothing but harm, he left for Paris in May 1890. On 27 July, at Auvers, he shot himself in the stomach, dying of the wound on 29 July.

These meagre and unhappy biographical data do not, however, truthfully represent van Gogh's real life in Provence, which was saved from being a sordid tragedy by the exemplary brilliance and profusion of the work he produced there. The anxieties, the fits, the quarrels with Gauguin, the self-inflicted wound, even the noisy ridicule with which the populace of Arles treated him after this incident, dwindle to insignificance when we reflect upon his paintings in this period – the studies of Provençal orchards, of the sunflowers, the cypresses, the olive trees and olive harvests, the garden of Saint-Paul, the bridge outside Arles, the portraits of the Zouave, of the *Berceuse*, of Roulin the postman, and of the Arlésiennes. Van Gogh's aim was the single one of conquering the obstacles which this strange countryside opposes to anyone attempting to interpret it: 'to get at its inner character,' as he wrote to Émile Bernard,* 'so that it's not something vaguely experienced, but the true soil of Provence'. 'It's a question of giving the sun and the blue sky their full force and brilliance,' he explains later in the same letter, 'and yet not omitting the fine aroma of wild thyme which pervades the hard-baked, often melancholy, landscape.' The innate melancholy of the Provençal landscape, and of much of its life, greatly impressed van Gogh, whose original notions on Provence had been formed, like those of most people of his generation, by the garrulous optimism and sentimentality of Alphonse Daudet's novels. 'I see nothing here of the southern gaiety that Daudet talks so much of,' he wrote, 'but on the contrary a sort of insipid airs and graces, a rather squalid casualness.'

In February 1888, when van Gogh stepped down from the train at Arles, the town and the surrounding country were under snow. Arles looked to him about the size of Mons or Breda, but the inhabitants – 'the Zouaves, the brothels, the adorable little Arlésiennes going to their first communion, the priest in his surplice, who looks like a dangerous rhinoceros, the people drinking absinthe' – all seemed to him infinitely alien, 'creatures from another world'. Even the lovely porch of Saint-Trophime, which he admired greatly, was 'cruel, monstrous', 'like a Chinese nightmare', and seemed the product of an age which he found as unsympathetic as that of the Roman world whose debris lay embedded about the old city's streets. The vaunted Arlesian beauties he thought disappointing, perhaps decadent: they must once have been handsome, but now they were 'more often like a Mignard than a Mantegna'. To his Dutch eyes Arles was, in its back streets, 'a filthy town', and he intelligently compared the derelict classical and medieval towns of Provence to those silent ports along the Zuyder Zee, the Dead Cities with their empty moss-grown wharves and echoing cold pavements of un-

*Lord, ed. cit., p. 92, letter from Saint-Paul-du-Mausolée of mid-October 1889.

trodden purple brick. But even in winter and under a coat of melting snow, the light and colour of Provence were a revelation to him.

'This country,' he wrote to Bernard shortly after his arrival in Provence,* 'seems to me as beautiful as Japan for clarity of atmosphere and gay colour effects. Water forms patches of lovely emerald or rich blue in the landscape, just as we see it in the crape-prints. The pale orange of the sunsets makes the fields appear blue. The sun is a splendid yellow.' He was already making studies; in early April he was hard at work on the ephemeral peach and pear-tree blossom of the Provençal orchards, painting ten pictures of these in as many days. In June he journeyed over the Camargue to the Saintes-Maries; in August, when everything turned 'old gold, bronze, copper . . . and this with the green azure of the sky blanched with heat', he began on the sunflowers. Everywhere he turned there were subjects, living or inanimate, crying out for interpretation and all illuminated by the sun – the elusive silvery olive trees against a yellow or a red-ochre soil, the cypresses, green-black and yet with the appearance of a flame. He did not seriously attack the cypresses until he was at Saint-Paul-du-Mausolée. 'When I had done those sunflowers,' he writes in a letter of this period, 'I looked for the opposite and yet the equivalent – it is the cypress.' For many months the cypress trees had been 'always occupying' his thoughts. He was astonished that they had not been painted as he saw them, as beautiful 'in line and proportion as an Egyptian obelisk'. 'It is a splash of *black* in a sunny landscape, but it is one of the most interesting of the black notes, and the most difficult to strike, that I can imagine. But then you must see them against the blue, *in* the blue rather.' The weeks at Saint-Rémy between his relapses passed in an intoxicating state of furious and energetic production.

Because of this immense creative energy, and because of the pictures that resulted from it, we have no right to sympathize with van Gogh, or to look on his time at Saint-Rémy, as one of his biographers† has done, as 'a nightmare'. He himself used the word

*First letter to Bernard from Arles, March 1888; Lord, p. 22.

†Julius Meier-Graeffe, *Vincent van Gogh*, English translation published by Medici Society, 1922. This standard work would seem to abound in misinterpretations of van Gogh's feelings and intentions.

'shipwreck' to describe what he felt about the end of the Provençal experiment, but with his extreme modesty, and his tremendous vision of what he knew that, given time, he could do, it is not odd that he belittled his own achievement in the south. At Saint-Paul, when he was not painting from nature, he was reading Shakespeare – particularly the historical plays – making versions, or as he called it, 'translating', from reproductions of pictures by Millet or from the lithographs of Gustave Doré, and studying his own illness by comparing it with those of the other patients, who were all kept in a state of complete indolence by Monsieur Peyron and the nuns, excellent women who knew nothing of occupational therapy, and who neither understood nor liked van Gogh's pictures, which they simply regarded as the proofs and products of his disease. A French writer who visited Saint-Paul-du-Mausolée after the First World War found that the mother superior then had been a young nun in the time of 'Monsieur Vincent', whom she perfectly remembered. He spent all his days painting, she said, and when he had an attack he would try to devour his paints and they would have to be taken away from him. Her only regret was that she had nothing of his to give to the inquirer; and when this honest Frenchman pointed out that he could not have accepted as a gift a picture which would be worth an untold sum, the old nun merely smiled and replied that disinterestedness was a basic Christian virtue, and that she would most willingly have given him any pictures or sketches that she had. Van Gogh, who, as a Dutch Protestant, did not altogether sympathize with the point of view of the nuns, would have subscribed to this comment: for he was incapable of sordid self-consideration, and was a being of exceptional generosity and singleness of mind.

There were one or two more distant chuckles of laughter behind the stone-pine trees that April morning, and I did not like to loiter in the garden of Saint-Paul-du-Mausolée. I had seen no lunatics – nor was it probable that if I did meet any they would look very different from one's own everyday circle of friends. But there was an atmosphere in the garden that made me feel uneasy, as though I were being watched; and on the way up from van Gogh's cell I had come upon an unpleasing stone head which I must have passed without noticing it before. This crudely carved bust, with the lolling mouth and the round eyes of an idiot, is no doubt the work of some talented former inmate of Saint-Paul. It stares out at you from a thicket of ivy. On the base of the plinth someone has cut, in large erratic capital letters, the terse and simple message: ALCOOL.

CHAPTER FIVE

AS I HAVE TRIED TO SHOW, THE TOWN of Saint-Rémy has many advantages as a place to stop in, and not least amongst these is the fact that the surrounding country provides an unending series of agreeable expeditions. You can wander in the ravines that van Gogh painted, or along the valley of Saint-Clerc where Gounod drifted as he composed *Mireille*: if you are very energetic you can walk to Maillane and see the Musée Mistral; you can hire a bicycle and visit Les Baux, or you can take the little train that goes to Tarascon to see the church of Sainte-Marthe and the castle of King René. If you have a car you are even better off, for every place of interest in this area of Provence lies within easy reach of Saint-Rémy. It is tempting to include Arles in this category, but though it is infinitely more pleasant to stay at Saint-Rémy, I do not think that you can see Arles properly without sleeping in it. Arles is a place you have to know well to like. At first sight, it seems inchoate, and sounds noisy; next it seems melancholy and deathly quiet. The long exterior boulevard by which you enter the town from Aix and Salon grinds with lorry traffic streaming westwards over the bombed Rhône bridge to Montpellier and Nîmes. This much-used thoroughfare gives you an illusion of commerce and modernity which the inside of the town does nothing to sustain. On this boulevard is situated the best hotel in Arles, the Jules César, installed in the gloomy corridors of a fifteenth-century Dominican monastery; but to my mind it is preferable to renounce the minimal comfort which the Jules César offers, and to put up at either the Hôtel du Forum, or like Stendhal, Mérimée and Henry James at the Hôtel du Nord-Pinus which, standing at right angles to it upon the Place du Forum, has an imposing piece of Roman monumental masonry embedded in its wall. At both of these hotels one is in the centre of Arles, and able to supplement routine sightseeing with personal observation of the city's rather torpid life.

Stendhal has called Arles 'a hole', only visited for its admirable monuments. Henry James, who saw the city in the rain, had much the same first impression. He found the streets 'like the streets of a village', with 'villainous sharp little stones' that made walking 'penitential'. The two hotels seemed shabby and unclean. The Alyscamps, though very romantic, were meagre and too close to an iron-foundry, while the superb and celebrated twelfth-century façade of Saint-Trophime was incongruous in a city of classical remains – 'It is very remarkable,' wrote Henry James, 'but I would rather it were in another place.' Only a moonlight walk in the antique theatre (then open day and night, now locked in behind iron railings, with an entrance fee to pay) mitigated his general sense of the discomforts of Arles. Yet in the end he came to like the place: 'As a city,' we read in *A Little Tour in France*, 'Arles quite misses its effect in every way; and if it is a charming place, as I think it is, I can hardly tell the reason why.' On further analysis he reduced the charm of Arles to two much-publicized features of this city, 'the straight-nosed Arlésiennes' (many of whom at that time still wore their elaborate local dress) and the Roman ruins. For the other components of this sad river city, James cared nothing at all.

For all its qualities of perception and sensibility, *A Little Tour in France* is in certain sections pernickety, and even old-maidish. For instance, it was surely purism on Henry James's part to regret the presence in Arles of one of the most splendid Romanesque churches in all France, for no town can consist of classic ruins only, and the details of the porch of Saint-Trophime, and of the capitals and pillars in the great cloister, are as remarkable as anything any city in Provence can show. Less spectacular, but also very lovely, is the town-hall of Arles, built to the designs of Mansart by one of his pupils. This town-hall, like the Renaissance belfry bearing the bronze figure of Mars, '*l'homme de bronze*', and like the seventeenth-century obelisk in the centre of the wide Place de la République, is an essential element of the city, and must not be ignored as one walks from the arena to the theatre or to the Tower of Roland and the Alyscamps (for like every town of this region, Arles is best visited on foot).

Although, as Henry James discovered, it is incredibly easy to get lost in what he termed 'the tortuous and featureless streets of Arles', there is one curious fact about all walks in that city – wherever you intend to go in it, you almost always end up unexpectedly at the amphitheatre. You may set off to cash a cheque at the Banque de France, which is in quite an opposite direction, or you may be trying for the fifteenth time to get someone to unlock the small museum in the former headquarters of the Knights of Malta, which contains indifferent paintings by the local eighteenth-century artist Réattu: sooner or later you find you have lost your way, you turn a corner, and there before you rise the gaunt walls of the arena, with its double tier of sixty arches, as white and vacant as the empty eye-sockets of sixty giant skulls.

Amphitheatres distinctly belong to that class of building that must be seen in use to be admired and understood. The vast elliptical one at Arles, naked to the sun and rain, open to the Provençal sky, seems meaningless when you first see it as a tourist, and buy your entrance ticket at the gate. It is best to wait for your next visit until the day of a bullfight, when the banks of seats are crammed with townspeople, and the sloping sides of the arena look as speckled as a pebbly beach. 'I have seen some bullfights in the arena,' van Gogh wrote to Bernard soon after his arrival in Arles, 'or rather they were sham fights, considering that the bulls were numerous, and no one fought them. But the crowd was magnificent, a huge multi-coloured mass piled up through two or three tiers of seats, with the effects of sun and shade and shadow cast by the enormous ring.'* We can no longer witness the fierce sanguinary contests of wild beasts and gladiators for which such arenas as those of Arles and Nîmes were built, nor can we enjoy any of the amenities provided for the audience in those antique days. For it may be presumed that like the people in the Colosseum at Rome, the Gaulish spectators at Arles were protected from the sun by awnings of purple cloth unfurled across the whole top of the arena. In Rome the steam of boiling saffron scented the air to counteract the reek of blood. The sand on the floor was

*Letters to E. Bernard, ed. Lord, p. 25.

startling white, or gleamed with metal shavings, or was dyed in bright colours by an admixture of tinted gravel. Today, at Arles and Nîmes, one must be ready to sit for many hours in the hot sun, drinking thin beer out of bottles sold at the booth near the entrance gate, and watching the gymnasts of the *ferrade* attempt to snatch a scarlet tassel from between a bull's horns with a steel comb held in the right hand. But the fact that the amphitheatre is full of people, and is being used, brings it to life, and gives it an atmosphere of purpose. For the rest one must imagine, as Henry James, leaning his elbows on the low parapet of the arena, says that one night he imagined, 'the murmurs and shudders, the thick voice of the circus that died away fifteen hundred years ago'. Prosper Mérimée also exercised his imagination upon the Arles arena, but his speculations were of a more technical nature. How, he wondered, were the people in the lowest seats protected from the wild beasts which could leap the wall dividing the floor of the arena from the podium? He supposed that those animals which could jump – lions, tigers, leopards – must have been secured with chains and weights, or rolled on to the scene in great iron cages. One is often reminded of this problem of Mérimée's, when one sees an angry little bull at Arles blunder over the wooden barrier in a fury, scattering the members of the audience, some of whom nimbly take refuge inside the arena itself until the animal is driven back to its stable.

Besides the arena, the Graeco-Roman theatre, the sarcophagi of the Alyscamps and the contents of the Musée Lapidaire, the other important classical debris of Arles comprise the baths of Constantine (an unrewarding brick ruin near the river Rhône) and the remains of a forum unearthed in the courtyard of the large Renaissance Hôtel Laval-Castellane under the auspices of the poet Mistral when he was forming the collections of the Muséon Arlatan which now entirely occupy this fine old palace. It is easy to scorn folk museums, places dedicated too often to the crafts not to the arts of a country, and offering you room after room unilluminated by a sense of beauty or one flash of individual talent. Yet some of them – the furniture museum at Hindeloopen on the Issel Meer, or the Frisian museum at Leeuwarden, or the splendidly housed collections by Bygdo in the suburbs of Oslo – can be extremely instructive. For lovers or students of Provence, the Muséon Arlatan (founded by Mistral with the money he gained from his Nobel Prize, and arranged with his own hands, many of the labels being inscribed in his neat writing) if somewhat musty is very interesting. There is, of course, a good deal of the usual truck of local museums – pieces of pottery, prehistoric arrow-heads, beards of withered hemp on spinning-wheels, dim and inde-cipherable coins – but there are also other collections lovingly and thoughtfully assembled – early examples of the *saintons*, or little Christmas figures, of Provence; musical instruments; Provençal games, charms and medals, paintings by local painters, and busts, photographs, manuscripts and other relics of the founders of the Félibrige. The last room of all contains two disturbing, life-size waxwork groups of Provençal scenes – a birth in a farmhouse, and the kitchen of the same at Christmas time. These great wax families with beady eyes, stiffly seated about a table laden with quantities of plaster food, have the nightmarish quality of all waxworks, but the two *tableaux*, and indeed almost all of the Muséon Arlatan, repay study, and serve as a sort of gloss, or illustrative commentary, on that most charming of autobiographies, Mistral's *Mes Origines*.

III

Like Saint-Rémy, Arles is at its prettiest in the months of spring, although in the autumn the city takes on a romantic sadness, as the cypresses along the Alyscamps sway when the mistral blows. Yet there are two or three days in the spring when it is wisest to avoid Arles. These fall in the last week in May, the time of the great pilgrimage and gipsy fêtes at the fortress-church of the Saintes-Maries-de-la-Mer, forty kilometres to the south-west across the burning plain of the Camargue. These Saintes-Maries festivities are complemented by an extensive commercial fair in Arles itself. During this period the city is crowded to confusion. Hotel rooms are un-obtainable, the streets are alive with pickpockets, the police demand your passport at any moment of the day. At these times, also, a rather self-conscious aspect is lent to Arles by the presence in its streets of girls in the old Arlesian dress. These descendants of those costumed and Grecian beauties whom the Blessingtons and their contemporaries admired are folksy and giggling: it seems to be only the aged women who can now wear the lovely full skirts, flowered aprons and ribboned bonnets with authority and ease. On these days, *danses folkloriques* are performed in the arena, when the bull-baiting is done. These dances must once have seemed as natural as the clothes of the girls who dance them; today they share the sadly artificial quality of all revivals, and are about as spontaneous as Morris dancing in Warwickshire. More romantic, because their occupations and functions are still genuine, are the lithe *gardians de la Camargue* who give a dashing show of horsemanship in the arena on these days. These Provençal cowboys, wearing check shirts and great felt cartwheel hats, ride the staunch cream-coloured horses of the Camargue with an air, and brandish a long trident in one hand. The *gardians'* business is to live in the sandy fastnesses of the Camargue, controlling the herds of tough black bulls drifting across that lonely plain which extends from the Petit-Rhône to the Rhône-Vif, and includes within its territory the ancient stranded seaports of Aigues-Mortes in the Languedoc and of Les Saintes-Maries-de-la-Mer in Provence. The lives of the *gardians* and of their wives seem unaffected by the advent of the motor-car, and we may suppose them to be as isolated as those of their predecessors described by Alphonse Daudet in his little novel *Le Trésor d'Arlatan*, a simple tale of mental corruption and suicide in the Camargue which no one going down into that mysterious region should omit to read.

The most vivacious incident of any festival at Arles however, is unquestionably the public dance held after dusk upon the Place du Forum, beneath plane trees strung with twinkling lights. In any Provençal town these open-air dances are delightful, but in Arles they seem especially so, possibly by the contrast or alternative they offer to the melancholy of the city's monuments and streets. Here you may watch, and if you will, participate, as the boys and girls of Arles, of the outlying villages and of the cabins and farmsteads of the Camargue dance with gusto to modern tunes. The Place du Forum is square, with cafés along three sides of it, and the Hôtel Nord-Pinus at its northern end. On a pedestal in front of this hotel, protected by a railing of tridents, and overlooking the dancing throng, stands a very large statue of the poet Frédéric Mistral in aqueous green bronze. He is shown in late middle age, bearded, wearing a wideawake hat and carrying his walking stick. A cloak is slung over his left arm, and the whole effect of the statue is to suggest that he has that moment come striding into Arles along the Maillane road. This statue, by a sculptor of Toulousain origin, Théodore Rivière, was unveiled in the poet's own presence with great pomp in May 1909.

IV

The inauguration of the statue of Mistral, forming part of the three-day celebrations that marked the fiftieth anniversary of the appearance of his first and most famous epic poem, *Mirèio*, was considered an event without any precedent in Provence, for the old man drove over from Maillane with his wife and his servant, 'Marie-du-Poète', to take the leading part in his own apotheosis. Even the most earnest of his admirers wondered how he would carry off a situation which many people might have found embarrassing. But at seventy-nine Mistral was as easy and natural as when he had impressed Lamartine as a youth. After listening to speeches in which he was praised to the skies, the old man mounted the rostrum, and with tears in his eyes told the audience that to thank them for all the beautiful things that had been said about him, he would repeat for them the Invocation from *Mirèio*. 'We seemed to be seeing, in the market-place of some Ionian town, Homer himself dominating the people by the majesty of his gestures and his words,' wrote one fervent witness. 'The faithful followers of the Master were reassured; as always he had hit upon the words and the attitude which were required.'

The unveiling of the Mistral statue was only one amidst a long series of festivities for the jubilee – the official opening of the Muséon Arlatan in the Hôtel de Laval, the costumed Bal Mireille, a display of rough-riding, the dancing of the farandole, and finally the open-air performance of Gounod's opera, *Mireille*, in the arena. Arles was crowded with people from every valley in Provence, from France generally, and also from abroad. The French government sent a representative to bestow the Grand Cross of the Legion of Honour on the poet. The French Academy, for which Mistral had declined to become a candidate, sent Vicomte de Vogüé. The Queen of Romania (the authoress of maxims under the name of Carmen Silva) sent

Prince Cantacuzene. The Queen of Portugal, President Theodore Roosevelt, and the Government of Sweden were also represented. The only unwelcome, and for some odd reason unexpected, visitor was the mistral itself, which began to howl through the decorated streets of the city on the night before the opening ceremonies, ripping to tatters the carefully-painted scenery for *Mireille* in the arena, and blowing flags hither and thither. Among his many superstitions Frédéric Mistral included one about the influence of names on events and he recognized the wind's sudden advent as an appropriate tribute to himself. From the windswept rostrum of the Place du Forum speaker after speaker praised the poet in Provençal and with all the true hyperbole of the Midi. The first appearance of *Mireille*, one speaker calmly declared, was 'not only a literary event, but also an historical one of greater importance for civilization than the outcome of a battle or the destiny of an empire'. To the eager, wind-blown audience on the Place du Forum this statement did not seem at all exaggerated. Nor, strangely enough, is it utterly absurd nor demonstrably untrue.

This deification of a living poet may seem to us to be in taste as questionable as that of the sea-green statue round which the ceremonies centred, especially if we recall how the townspeople of Arles had scoffed at van Gogh twenty years earlier. The whole Félibrean movement, with its emphasis on an artificial language, its desperate attempts to preserve local costume, its idealization of the troubadours' way of life, *Le Gai-Savoir*, its rather smug exuberance and self-satisfaction, can seem insufferably histrionic, while those photographs of the plump-faced members of the Félibrige and of their wives dressed in Arlesian costumes in which the Muséon Arlatan abounds do not increase one's sympathy with that movement. But you must not be deterred by these appearances, for the Mistral cult is one which every serious traveller in Provence must tackle and understand.

I was told, one morning at Cambridge, by an eminent don, that no one should go to Provence without having read Mistral's *Pouèmo dou Rose* or *Le Poème du Rhône*. This is the one species of advice it is always safe to follow, so when I returned to London I bought a copy of that poem, and I read it while I was ill with measles, one hot July, in an hotel in Arles. I also purchased from the small bookshop behind the town-hall a copy of the poet's autobiography, *Mes Origines*, and a volume of *Mirèio* in the compact edition devised by the poet himself, with the Provençal verse on one page and his own French prose translation on the other. *Mirèio* and the *Poème du Rhône* are respectively the earliest and the latest of Mistral's four great epics: *Mes Origines* is his last work of all. These two poems contain more realism and less fantasy than the intervening *Calendau*, a tale of a fisherman of Cassis, and *Nerto*, a fairy story about the caves beneath the mountains of the Alpilles. All four epics have their inspiration in common – for they originate in, and most movingly express, Mistral's passionate devotion to his own country. His descriptions of the Provençal landscape – the vineyards, the plains, the lilac mountains, the tumbled villages, towns, farmhouses, antique ruins and aqueducts of the country about Arles and Saint-Rémy, Avignon and Beaucaire – glow and glimmer through the verse. Critics have observed that the heroes and heroines of Mistral's epics – often enough boys and girls of thirteen or fourteen years of age – never hold the front of the stage for a whole poem, and that their psychology is uncomplicated and their emotions simple. Although this one-dimensional quality of Mistral's characters has been exaggerated – at times his peasant girls sing out their love with the abandon of a Wagnerian heroine – it seems likely that the poet was always more interested in the scenes he was describing than in the imaginary persons whom he placed in them. As brilliant as a summer's morning in the Vaucluse, Mistral's landscape-painting is far more than a mere backcloth to the tales his epics tell. It forms, as it were, the core of the poems, the reason perhaps for their existing at all. Epic in form and in intention, Mistral's verse becomes lyrical when he is writing of Provence, and his poems should be read during, and not before, a first journey through the country he describes. Only thus can we respond to the drum-taps of excitement with which the poet names some crag near Les Baux, or writes of Martigues with its boats laden with gleaming mackerel, or when he recounts the flight of the dying Mirèio over the Camargue to pray before the relics at the Saintes-Maries. The autobiographical prose work, *Mes Origines*, on the other hand, provides the best preparation for Provence I know. It is unsurpassed for this purpose by any set guide or travel-book yet written on Provence.

This account of Mistral's boyhood and youth from his birth in 1830 to the triumphant publication of *Mirèio* in 1859 has qualities of warmth and conviction which place it high in that absorbing category of memoirs, those of poets and writers. The rural tranquillity of the opening chapters of *Mes Origines* remind us of those of an earlier French poet's reminiscences – the *Mémoires* which Marmontel wrote for his children in his old age. There is the same genial lucidity about the two accounts of childhood and early schooling – Marmontel in the torrential valleys of the Dordogne, Mistral in the balmy Provençal plain near Saint-Rémy. Both poets were influenced in their early years by their native landscape; but whereas Marmontel went to Paris and obtained the patronage of Monsieur de la Poplinière and Madame de Pompadour, Frédéric Mistral neither sought nor wished for metropolitan success, and was content to spend his long life quietly and happily in Provence, in the very village community into which he had been born. Occasionally he would visit Paris. He journeyed once, with his wife, to Italy. But Mistral was not happy away from Provence, and there he lived out his dedicated life, devoted to the creation – or as he and his fellow workers liked to call it – the 'revival' of a written form of the *langue d'oc*, and to the service of his country-people in Provence. There are few lives of great writers, perhaps few recorded lives of human beings, as fortunate and enviable as that of Frédéric Mistral, voluntarily circumscribed within the limits of the halcyon landscape into which he had had the superlative good fortune to be born.

In an English study of Mistral's verse, published in 1937,* an intelligent attempt is made to isolate the poet from his Provençal background, and to place him beside Homer, Virgil and Dante. His claims to this high position must be a matter for critical opinion, but the attempt (provoked by the jealous idolatry with which Mistral has been regarded in Provence) puts him quite out of perspective. For though much of his popularity in his lifetime was due to the beauty of his verse, it was the fact that he alone had produced masterpieces in the ancient tongue that assured his position in Provence. When, with Roumanille and the five other founders of the Félibrige, Mistral in 1854 established the new brotherhood dedicated to the revival of

Dreamer and Striver: The Poetry of Frédéric Mistral, by C.M. Girdlestone (Methuen, 1937).

a written *langue d'oc*, and to the preservation of old Provençal customs and ways, no one could tell just how influential the movement might or might not become. Owing to Mistral it went very far indeed. It was he who made Provence race-conscious, and restored to the people a sense of nationality that they had forgotten for five hundred years. For superficial reasons, Mistral has been compared to Burns, yet it is Sir Walter Scott that he most closely resembles, since he did for Provence in the second half of the nine-teenth century what Sir Walter had done for Scotland in its first three decades. To Mistral western Provence was enchanted ground. He had felt for it from childhood just as violently as Sir Walter had felt for the Border country, and like him he harvested the folk-tales, compounds of historic incident and pure legend, and wove his poems from them, peopling a whole countryside with imaginary characters, witches, magicians, lovers and antique heroes. He had the same burning regional patriotism as Sir Walter, the same wildly romantic reactions to some ruined keep or Roman stone. As Scott cared for the old Border ballads, so Mistral cared for the traditional love-songs of Provence, in many of which could be heard echoes of the melodies of the troubadours. In spite of the popularity of the *Provençal Almanach* which he published annually and of the great dictionary of Provençal which it took him thirteen laborious years to construct, Frédéric Mistral failed to achieve his ideal of making the peasantry of Provence thirsty for literature in their own tongue. But he did, like Scott, succeed in making a whole countryside vocal, and in forcing upon the attention of the outside world the existence of Provence, and its intense individuality. The political, allegedly separatist, tend-encies of the Félibrean movement, for some years suspect to the government of the French Republic, proved harmless and in-conclusive: yet at his death in 1914 Frédéric Mistral left Provence more aware of itself, and more celebrated, than it had been for many hundred years. 'A synthesis of local forces', Mistral clearly deserved the honour and gratitude which he has been lavishly accorded in Provence.

Arles, with its Rivière statue, its Provençal museum and tradition of Félibrean jollities, is an important focal point of the Mistral cult, but the real centre of this is Maillane by Saint-Rémy. The Mas du Juge, the long, comfortable, two-storeyed farmhouse in which Frédéric Mistral was born in September 1830, is near Maillane, and in the actual village the two other houses of the poet still stand: the Maison au Lézard which he inhabited from 1855 until his marriage in 1876, and the villa which he built for himself and his wife in that year and where they lived tranquilly up to his death just before the declaration of the First World War. '*Maillane! Un jour Maillane voudra dire Mistral, comme les Charmettes ou Vevey veulent dire Jean-Jacques,*' wrote the composer Charles Gounod to his wife in March 1863.

The seven kilometres of road that lead from Saint-Rémy to Maillane wind through cultivated level country of exceptional beauty. The vines are low upon the ground, hedgerows of white hawthorn flower rustle with long grasses through which lizards flash, and the elms and the plane trees and the fruit trees and the black-green cypresses seem less to be growing from the earth than floating in the sky. There are whole areas of France in which one is more conscious of the sky than one ever becomes anywhere in England, except perhaps in the wide Weald of Kent. On the plain of Maillane and Saint-Rémy the sky can sometimes seem more important than the earth, for here above the low green land the dawns and sunsets quiver – magenta changing to pale apple green, scarlet to deep yellow – and at midday the sky is as blue as in the tropics, and every tree and church-tower seems to be visible not against the blue, but, as van Gogh tried to explain, within or through it. On the way to Maillane you pass an iron cross upon the bank of the rivulet than runs beside the road; this cross marks the entrance to the Mas du Juge, the whitewashed farmstead where in a white-curtained bed in the alcove of a plain airy room with a floor of polished reddish tiles, Madame Mistral gave birth to her famous son.

Maillane itself, when you reach it, is a small and amiable place, with an unpretentious country church in which the poet was baptized. In a street not far from the church is the House of the Lizard, used by Mistral and his mother after the father's death in

1855. Here Mistral completed *Mirèio*, *Calendau* and *Les Isclo d'Or*. Opposite this house, which takes it name from a sundial with a lizard carved over the lintel of the front door, is the Muséon Frédéric Mistral, as a tin plaque upon its garden wall informs you. This museum is installed in the banal villa which Mistral built as a home for himself and his Dijonnaise wife whom he married in 1876 when he was approaching fifty, and she nineteen. Even when new this house was sadly admitted by some of his admirers to be 'the least characteristic' of the three in which he lived and wrote, for while officially described as 'half town-house, half Provençal farm', it is as a matter of fact a villa in the Second Empire manner, set behind a high garden wall with spikes on top of it, and altogether indistinguishable from any other small French suburban building of its epoch. To Mistral the merit of the villa was its garden and its privacy – for the lizard house was on the street, and had no flowers at all. The garden is small, rather wild, and endearing. A friend of Mistral's called it 'the garden of a priest or of a poet', and praised its lack of pomposity and style, but it is really the garden of a romantic, with wandering pathways, many laurels and myrtles, roses that bloom from early spring into the autumn, and beds of verbena. The poet and his wife were perfectly satisfied with it, and here he would genially receive the admirers who converged upon him from all parts of France and of the world. 'We went more than once to see the great man in his garden at Maillane, a pleasant place surrounding a cool, quiet villa, where the poet lives with his young wife,' wrote an English traveller in 1892. 'It is the only house of any pretensions in Maillane, and to the good people of the commune Monsieur Mistral is both the poet and the squire. He comes out to receive you – a strikingly handsome man with a beautiful voice...much like Buffalo Bill in his appearance.'* Madame Darmesteter saw a good deal of the Mistrals, who took her to the races at Saint-Rémy. '*Regardez nos fillettes*,' the poet said to her, pointing to the girls of Maillane and Tarascon, Avignon and Arles, in their full black skirts, white tulle fichus, pointed shawls and flowered aprons: '*On dirait des statues grecques*.'

Today the hospitable villa at Maillane is as dead as every other

Contemporary Review, vol. cit.

museum-house of its kind, whether it be the sad and stuffy apartments of the Lamartines at the Château de Saint-Point, or the gaunt rooms of the Carlyles in Cheyne Row. To try to preserve a room or a house exactly as its defunct owner left it defeats all reverent purpose, and creates a horrifying atmosphere of mortality and decay. It is as though the clothes and intimate possessions of the dead died with them; and by leaving each chair in place, each pipe upon its rack, the pious curators of the Mistral villa present us with an architectural mummy which makes us shiver on the hottest summer's day. The inside of the house it seems was always painfully brown: the flowered wallpapers are brown and beige, the bookcases mahogany, the chairs the same. The bedrooms, simple to the point of austerity, look sepulchral, but far too private, and make you feel that you intrude. The study in which Mistral wrote is chiefly notable for being crowded with medals, drawings, photographs, busts and maquettes of the poet, who evidently shared that enthusiasm for his own handsome features which also obsessed Alphonse de Lamartine. The whole house is as sympathetic and as cosy as a coffin, and it is with a tremor of relief and new vitality that one hastens out of it again into the garden, into the sunlight and the country Mistral loved.

VI

Born two months after the fall of Charles X and the setting up of the July Monarchy, Frédéric Mistral was the son of the second marriage of an old-fashioned, dignified and well-to-do peasant farmer, owner of the Mas du Juge, a good small property situated five kilometres from Saint-Rémy and two from the little commune of Maillane. His mother, daughter of a mayor of Maillane, was a country girl of somewhat lower social status than her husband. She was also very much younger than he. Both parents were determined that their son should have a modern education, superior to that which they had themselves been given. Madame Mistral, whose Christian name was prettily contracted into 'Delaide', was a very simple woman whom Lamartine chose later to acclaim as *'cette belle veuve Arlésienne, semblable aux heroines de la Bible et de l'Odyssée'*. Like her husband and all his family, Madame Mistral spoke by choice and habit the

Provençal of Saint-Rémy. She was religious, and also imbued with all the harmless and evocative superstitions of the Arlesian countryside. These she handed on to her son, who remained convinced throughout his life that the world was governed by mysterious and often mystic laws, and who could, if challenged, produce disquieting evidence of coincidences and inexplicable turns of fate which he had experienced in his own life. Frédéric's imagination was equally affected by the legends his mother and the other village women repeated to him. Some of these legends – that, for example, of the procession of the Three Kings to Maillane at Epiphany, which would send the small children of the village scampering along the Arles road before dusk in the hope of meeting the oriental cortège, clutching in their hands cakes for the kings, figs for their pages, and hay for their camels – were Christian. Others, like those of the malign activities of the Esprit Fantastique – a Provençal Puck, or Lob-lie-by-the-Fire – probably dated from before the Christian era.

These tales and legends, and the devotion to Provence embodied in them, filled the boy's mind while he was being educated, first as a boarder at an eccentric establishment vaguely conducted on a basis of barter by a Monsieur Donnat, in the nearby derelict abbey of Saint-Michel-de-Frigolet, and later at the two lycées which he successively attended in Avignon. It was at Avignon (the poet wrote in a private letter*), that he first learned with anger that he was expected to speak, and do his work, in French. He realized that all he loved most – the traditions, customs, language and legends of old Provence – was turned to ridicule by people who talked French, and looked to Paris as their capital. Mistral felt humiliated – 'not only for myself,' he wrote, 'but for my family and my race' – and swore to revenge himself by restoring its full vigour to 'the sacrosanct maternal tongue', taking an oath that he would never enter any profession obliging him to use the foreign and imposed language.

At the lycée of Monsieur Dupuy, the second of those he attended at Avignon, Mistral met Joseph Roumanille, a native of Saint-Rémy, twelve years his senior, and attached to the school as an usher.

*Letter of 1867 to S.B. Gaut, director of the *Mémorial d'Aix*, published in 1913 by J. Charles-Roux in his *Le Jubilé de Frédéric Mistral* (Blond et Cie., Paris, 1913). This book contains many fascinating photographs.

Roumanille, who was already experimenting with Provençal verse, and studying *Les Noëls de Saboly** at the public library in Avignon, caught the boy scribbling during vespers on a Sunday evening in the gloomy Carmelite church of Saint-Symphorien on the Place des Carmes. Confiscating the paper, he found it to be the draft of a Provençal translation of the penitential psalms; and in spite of the difference of age, Roumanille and Mistral made friends, and, together with another founder member of the Félibrige who was then also a student at the lycée, Anselme Mathieu, began to discuss plans for a Provençal renaissance. Since the time of Louis XIV, the old *langue d'oc* had gradually lost its traditional written form. The few meridional poets who had continued to use it as a means of expression had, through carelessness and also through ignorance, accepted the French orthography, and embroidered the older language with oddities and arbitrary additions of their own. The aim of Mistral and Roumanille was to clear away these accretions, and restore to the *langue d'oc* its ancient lustre and simplicity. In achieving this – and there can be no question that they did largely achieve it – they tended to place an undue emphasis upon the dialects of their own district, and later critics of the movement accused them of constructing a written language out of the peasant patois of the fields round Saint-Rémy. Roumanille's father was a gardener of that town, and it is related that one day when Joseph, who had originally written verses in French, was repeating some of these to his friends, the gardener's wife burst into tears because she could not understand the beautiful things her son was saying. This incident decided Joseph Roumanille to write only in Provençal and enabled the Félibres (who were never averse to sentiment) to claim that the Provençal Renaissance was 'born of a mother's tear'.

After a period of law studies at Aix-en-Provence, Frédéric Mistral returned to Maillane to write. In May 1854 – *'en pleine primavère de*

---

*Nicholas Saboly, born at Monteux in the Comtat Venaissin in 1614, was educated by the Jesuits of Carpentras, ordained priest at the age of twenty-one, and became organist at Carpentras Cathedral, moving in 1643 to Avignon. 'A golden link in the chain which unites Mistral to the troubadours', Saboly was the author of a long series of fantastic, simple and popular poems and songs in honour of the Nativity. A *Recueil des noëls provençaux, composez par le Sr Nicolas Saboly, Beneficiere and Maître de Musique de l'église de St Pierre d'Avignon* was published at Avignon in 1699. All Saboly's poems were in Provençal.

la vie et de l'an', as he writes in *Mes Origines* – Mistral, Roumanille, Mathieu, Aubanel and three more young poets met together at the Château de Fontségugne, near Avignon, and there founded the Félibrige. Although the name *félibre* was chosen with care, none of them could explain either its precise derivation, or just what it meant. It was the expression used in a traditional folk-song of Maillane upon the Seven Sorrows of Our Lady, and it occurred in a passage describing her discovery of Christ in the temple, disputing *'avec les sept* félibres *de la Loi'*. The word was immediately appropriated by the seven poets, who began to manufacture various derivatives from it – *Félibrige, félibréen, félibresse*, and so on. This account, given frankly by Mistral in his memoirs, was often confirmed by him in conversation: 'I ventured to ask him the meaning of the name, which is a puzzle not to philologists alone', wrote Madame Darmesteter in 1892. 'He confessed it had no particular meaning ... No one knew precisely what the word designed – so much the greater its charm, its suggestiveness!'

In 1856, Mistral, at work on *Mirèio*, paid his first visit to Paris. Before returning south he was taken by Adolphe Dumas to visit Lamartine, who was captivated by the beauty, modesty and simplicity of the youth, and rather impressed by the lyrics which Mistral repeated to him. When *Mirèio* appeared three years later, the first copy was dispatched to Lamartine. The old poet was astounded by the warmth and beauty of this epic verse. He devoted an article to it in the *Cours Familier de Littérature* from which he was then trying to make a living. *'J'ai crié comme vous,'* he wrote to a friend, *'C'est Homère!'*

With the appearance and spontaneous success of *Mirèio*, Mistral's position was assured; the rest of his long life was spent in composing three more epics, the dictionary, *Les Îles d'Or*, and many other minor poems. With his colleagues he worked away at the revival of Provençal language and nationalism, becoming first a popular, then an almost legendary, character throughout Provence. Foreigners visiting Avignon in the nineties found their cabbies stopping in the middle of the street to point out members of the Félibrige to them: 'Look at that, monsieur!' the cabman would say, 'Look at him! He's a poet!' as Félix Gras or Roumanille or Aubanel strolled by. 'Every person of every degree treasures some little speech or anecdote concerning Monsieur Mistral, the hero of the place', a visitor recorded.

We must not allow the fame and popularity of Frédéric Mistral, or the photographs and the statuettes, to obscure for us the extraordinary simple charm which he radiated when alive, and which much of his work transmits to us today. A good clear glimpse of the poet at home in the Maison du Lézard is to be found in the correspondence of Charles Gounod, who went down from Paris in 1863 to see the poet, with the intention of writing an opera from *Mirèio*. '*Je le tiens enfin,*' he wrote to his wife, '*ce beau et bon Mistral tant rêvé, tant cherché et tant desiré.*' He was 'enchanted' by Mistral, on whom God seemed to have showered all His gifts – goodness, simplicity, beauty, generosity. His personality was like his style – pure and primitive. Gounod, who knew that works of art are the result of long, hard, lonely application, and who believed 'continuity' to be the major element in creative work, settled in happy isolation at Saint-Rémy, far away from the interruptions of Paris, yet near enough to Mistral to be able to see him whenever he wished. Together they would walk in the country round Saint-Rémy, picking violets and talking of the progress of the opera and of Mistral's own work. It was March, but the spring was warm and sparkling. Gounod would sit at an open window of the hotel, looking out on the Provençal sunset and writing. 'Near here, twenty minutes from Saint-Rémy, there is the most beautiful mountain valley that you could see anywhere: it is pure Italy; it is even Greece,' he wrote, and again, 'This is the Italy of France, how right I was to settle here.'

On Gounod's second day in Provence, Mistral had taken him on foot from Maillane to Les Baux, through country which seemed to the composer 'a marvel of savagery'. 'The crags are one with the feudal and medieval ruins,' he wrote excitedly. He had stood with Mistral on the summits of Les Baux and gazed down across the coloured plains of the Crau and the Camargue to the distant sea. 'The panorama,' he declared, 'is more vast than that of the Roman Campagna, and terrifyingly stern.'

CHAPTER SIX

I

'THE CASTLE,' WROTE JOHN ADDINGTON SYMONDS, of the Château des Baux, 'looks out across a vast extent of plain over Arles, the stagnant Rhône, the Camargue, and the salt pools of the lingering sea.' A careful and fastidious writer, Symonds had a rare descriptive gift. The river Rhône, of course, by no means stagnates, nor does the Mediterranean 'linger' on that stony shore; but seen from the lofty distance of Les Baux both seem to do so. Also, Symonds was not afraid of the pathetic fallacy: 'Far and near, upon desolate hillside and sandy plain,' (he writes of nearing Avignon one February, when the mistral blew) 'the scanty trees are bent sideways, the crumbling castle turrets shivering like bleached skeletons in the dry ungenial air.' 'On flies the raft, the tall reeds rustle, and the cypress sleeps,' he writes musically of the progress past a solitary cypress on the Rhône bank, of a long raft 'guided by a score of men', in a piece of prose as slight and clear as an incident recorded upon a Japanese screen. He remarks the strange symmetrical appearance of the 'domed summer clouds' sailing above the Pont du Gard, and, seen through its arches, 'comprehended in the gigantic span of their perfect semicircles'. He calls the plain of Avignon 'wind-tormented' and the feudal seigneurs of Les Baux 'a comet race' –

here they lived and flourished, these feudal princes, bearing for their ensign a silver comet of sixteen rays upon a field of gules – themselves a comet race, baleful to the neighbouring lowlands, blazing with lurid splendour over wide tracts of country, a burning, raging, fiery-souled, swift-handed tribe ... until, in the sixteenth century, they were burned out, and nothing remained but cinders – these broken ruins of their eyrie, and some outworn and dusty titles.*

Symonds was still quite a young man when he first travelled in

*See the chapter 'Old Towns of Provence' in J.A. Symond's *Sketches and Studies in Italy and Greece: First Series* (reprinted by John Murray, 1933).

Provence, on his way to Italy, in February 1866. He admired the 'amethyst' water of Petrarch's grotto at Vaucluse, and he gathered early violets in the Roman theatre of Orange. In October 1867 he came through Provence again, going this time from Glion in French Switzerland to Cannes. Travelling comfortably with their child, its nurse and a footman, Mr and Mrs Symonds journeyed 'slowly in wet autumn weather' through Avignon, Nîmes and Arles, 'seeing much and profiting by what we saw'. Like other travellers of their day, the Symondses relied on Murray's guide to tell them what was profitable to see, and like all travellers of every era they did not always agree with what their guide-book told them. 'Murray is wrong,' wrote Symonds, discussing Les Baux, 'in calling the place a medieval town in its original state, for anything more purely ruinous, more like a decayed old cheese, cannot possibly be conceived. The living only inhabit the tombs of the dead.' A modern visitor may likewise feel, with disappointment, that the raptures of the present-day *Guide Bleu* over this ruined fortress are no less exaggerated. For, urging its readers to inspect Les Baux, the *Guide* flings moderation to the winds, and in place of the civil, impersonal adviser, to whose monotony of sober facts and dates we are accustomed, and whose small print and seemingly adhesive pages have tried our patience in crypt and forum, in tenebrous cloister and beneath some isolated monumental arch, we find ourselves mounting the harsh ascent to the derelict Valhalla of Provence in lyrical company. 'One cannot recommend too strongly a night passed at Les Baux,' the little book proclaims, insisting that we do not quit the mountain-top without 'the unforgettable souvenir' of Les Baux at sundown, and of a moonlit ramble through the ruined streets to the ruined castle's ruined walls. 'Artists and archaeologists,' the *Guide Bleu* reminds us, love 'to wander where their fancy leads them through the ruins of this once opulent city.' Yet all but the nimblest and most wary people of any profession would find such rambling perilous by night, for the soft calcareous limestone out of which the crumbling houses seem to grow is pitted with yawning caves and concealed cellars, while whole portions of the castle ruins have no floor at all, and you may peer down through roofless dungeons on to the bleak grey rocks of the valley beneath. A thousand metres above the level of the sea, the narrow precipices of Les Baux are haunted by the mistral, which howls across the ruins and strives to blow one off the edge into the night.

Yet in some ways the *Guide Bleu* is not wrong: at least one visit to Les Baux should be made by night, though whether it is not better to sleep in the hotel at Saint-Rémy rather than in one of those in the ruined citadel must remain a matter of personal taste. Having tried both experiments, I would myself choose Saint-Rémy for several reasons: though the new hotel at Les Baux, with a blue swimming-pool before it and delicious food, is comfortable and even luxurious. At night Les Baux is terrifyingly lonely: the midnight silence is shattered merely by the baying of some stray dog at the moon, or by the echo of a church bell as the church clock strikes the hour. Below you in the valley you can hear the gross coarse croaking of the bull-frogs in the ponds. The citadel of Les Baux – the climbing crooked lanes of empty houses, the unencumbered plateau where the castle halls once stood, the flat terrace outside the church of Saint-Vincent, the little tufted graveyard cluttered with iron monuments and wreaths of coloured beads – lies silent on its promontory, jutting up in a night sky hooped with stars. At full moon the shadows of the broken houses and the rocks into which they are built look as black and solid as the masonry itself: the turf, and the stony soil with its sparse clumps of lavender and small rosettes of rock-plants, lies bright blue in the moonlight. Standing in the graveyard, or on the rocks beside it, you can gaze down across the whole expanse of the Crau and the Camargue, and beyond these at the sea, a distant gleaming thread, and on the horizon, a sparkle from the lamps and windows of the hamlet of the Saintes-Maries. Nearer, and eastward, the lights of Arles seem spattered on the darkness like a shell-burst in the sky.

II

The inaccessible position of Les Baux, its striking history and its deserted site, combine to give that place an air of high romance which close examination proves invalid. Anyone who has had the task of writing a biography from family papers, or has spent time in sorting from some old box or chest of drawers the letters and the relics – the private notes, the locks of hair – of an earlier generation, knows the feeling of overwhelming nausea and exhaustion which will descend upon you without warning and in the midst of the most fascinating work. At such moments the past seems oppressively dead, and history appears a charnel-house. This transitory mood of revulsion can be induced by certain places as well as by certain ploys. Les Baux is one of these.

First mentioned in a document in AD 981, the castle of the Seigneurs des Baux, with its satellite township, was ambitiously placed upon a lofty spur of the Alpilles which jutted southwards towards the sea. The strategic element of this situation is further emphasized by the fact that its ruins are almost invisible from the two valley roads by which you can approach Les Baux. The castle and the other buildings, including the sixteenth-century town houses of the Porcelets, the Manvilles, and other families, were naturally built of local stone, and seem today to fade into the rocks on which they stand. As one toils upwards to Les Baux on a grilling summer's day, the limestone crags above one look as wild and as bare of buildings as any of the Alpilles' adjacent peaks: then gradually the untidy silhouettes of broken fortifications become visible, you can make out an archway here, turrets and a doorway there, gaping windows, the bell-tower of a church. By the time you reach the entrance to the village, you have the impression that the whole place is inhabited and full of life; but when, after crossing a car-park and skirting a postcard booth, you begin walking up the sinuous, straggling Grande Rue you find a succession of empty houses on either hand. A few of these houses have lately been restored, but the majority are ruinous. All are open to inspection and seem like a street of bombed dwellings at some macabre universal exhibition or pacifist world's fair. You walk in and out of doorways without doors, and poke your head through window-frames that have no glass. At the farther end of the long main street you emerge upon a grassy plateau, its surface humped with ruined foundations: here in hot weather you may lie or sit upon the ground, absorbing the great shining breadth of view. Below this plateau, and in the very face of the cliff that carries it, are small terraces with more houses, hewn out of the rock, fronting on to them. Here again the view over the valley is superb; but, like many of the ruins of Les Baux, these rock houses are indescribably squalid, hovels with walls covered in tourists' names and graffiti, their floors clotted with filth, and stinking of urine.

Much nonsense has been written of Les Baux. It has been called a Provençal Pompeii, 'a Herculaneum without its lava'. In fact this tiny commune, which is centred round the remnants of a feudal castle destroyed at Richelieu's orders in 1631, and now numbers some two hundred inhabitants, can never at its most opulent have contained more than three thousand persons. The great castle of Les Baux was a spacious and important fortified building – as large, some estimates suggest, as the Palace of the Popes at Avignon – and the main residence (and refuge) of one of the most powerful feudal dynasties of Provence, a family who claimed descent from Balthasar, one of the Magi, and bore the Star in the East in silver as their coat of arms. Possessors of great territories and many towns collected by alliance, inheritance, murder, treachery and conquest, the Seigneurs des Baux spent their time (like the Comtes de Forcalquier and other medieval members of the Provençal nobility) in small local wars, and in taking sides in the perennial struggle between the Toulouse and the Barcelona branches of the rulers of Provence. These wars, conducted from such strongholds as Les Baux, formed the heroic themes for the ballads of the troubadours and minstrels who frequented these nobles' courts. The troubadour Elias de Barjols, for instance, is known to have composed a work now lost celebrating the wars of the *Baussanques* or seigneurs of Les Baux. The Provençal troubadours likewise gave voice and rhythmic literary form to that complicated official love-making, those *protocolaire* attachments and conventions of undying devotion with which, shut aloft in their tapestried castles on some windy hilltop like Vaison or Les Baux, the ladies of these lords passed their time, alleviating with a calculated frivolity lives of sumptuous piety which often ended in an elegant retirement from the world to the convent of the noble Dames at Aix. When Adelicia des Baux, the last of her line, died in the great chamber of the castle in 1426, she left behind no fewer than eight pearl-studded rosaries, together with many illuminated Books of Hours and precious missals bound in gold and pearls. It is indeed in the illuminated manuscripts of the fourteenth and fifteenth centuries that we can best get a glimpse of the rich trappings of life at a castle like Les Baux: for existence on this desolate crag, overlooking the marshes of the Crau and the Camargue yet within reach of Papal Avignon, was as luxurious as that of Aquitaine or Normandy, or of the city-states of contemporary Italy. Two centuries before, Eleanor, daughter of Raymond-Béranger V of Provence, and 'perhaps the most unpopular queen that ever presided over the court of England', had made herself notorious in her adopted country by her rapacity and luxury, and by the sybaritic state which she, her numerous relatives, and her swarming Provençal attendants kept there; and there is no reason to suppose that the luxurious standards of the Provençal nobility in the thirteenth century had been lowered in the fifteenth. The inventory taken at the death of Adelicia des Baux (an event marked by the apparition in her death-chamber of the Star of the East, which hovered shimmering above her bed) shows that she lived in considerable comfort – with oriental carpets on the floors, tapestries upon the walls, great tables and cedar-lined chests, gold and silver candlesticks and much other plate. The appurtenances of her chapel, which was hung with tapestries portraying the story of the Magi, were of richly jewelled and enamelled gold. Her halls and corridors were decorated with arms and armour, much of it obsolete. The kitchens and pantries were stocked with stores and wine, and herds of cattle, sheep and pigs were kept in the fields beside the forests below the castle rock. Medieval and early Renaissance life is curiously hard for us to picture, and when we enter the dusty honeycomb streets and gardens of Les Baux, and gaze up at the birds' nests in the walls of the castle rooms, the idea that this place was for centuries the scene of a small, self-contained and highly cultivated court seems not less but more improbable and remote.

Prosper Mérimée, who visited Les Baux during his official journey through Provence in 1834, found that the 'spectacle ... of this habitable town which is uninhabited' appealed more strongly to his imagination than that of some Roman city of which nothing but the substructure remains. 'It is,' he noted, 'all the difference between a catastrophe one reads about and a disaster which one witnesses.' Mérimée saw no building at Les Baux that seemed to him previous in date to the twelfth century; the majority of the houses he thought of the period of the Renaissance. In his time the town, which he wrongly judged could in its heyday have sheltered six thousand people, was used only by a handful of beggars and gipsy squatters.

On one of the houses Mérimée observed a postbox hanging: 'But who,' he asked, 'can ever write a letter to Les Baux?'

III

When, with the death of Adelicia des Baux in 1426, this powerful family became extinct, the contents of the castle in the Alpilles were dispersed. A part was sold. A part was sent, in accordance with her wishes, to the Bishop of Tortosa. The rest was loaded on to ox-wagons and taken across country to the great Angevin stronghold at Tarascon on the Rhône's eastern bank. This splendid castle, which you pass as you enter Provence from the west, stands on a rock rising straight from the waters of the Rhône. It bears the same magical relation to that river which the castle of Chillon bears to Lac Leman, and like Chillon its reflection may be seen shining in the surface of the water on still days.

Built in the late fourteenth century by Louis II of Provence, King of Sicily, and completed fifty years afterwards by his son, the 'good King' René, the castle of Tarascon ranks second only to the palace at Avignon amongst the surviving secular buildings of the Middle Ages in Provence. It is also one of the most important and best preserved fifteenth-century castles in all France. Used from the sixteenth century until quite lately as a prison* – just as the Palace of the Popes served for generations as barracks for Moroccan troops – the castle of Tarascon no doubt owes the excellent state of its walls and fortifications to this fact. Somewhat restored before it was opened to the public in 1926, the castle is, in its exterior, imposing and func-tional – a solid, yellow, square-built edifice with fat turrets at the four corners, castellations, machicolated galleries, and, on the river side, large windows caged by iron grilles; it seems a castle in some miniature illustration to the chronicles of Froissart. The inner court,

*On the walls of many of the rooms in the castle are the names of eighteenth-century English prisoners during the French wars, 'lightermen' from London, Hull, etc., and many rhyming inscriptions, such as one of 1778:

> Here is 3 Davids in one mess
> Prisoners we are in Distress
> By the French we was caught
> And to this prison we was brought.

with an elaborate spiral staircase, and floriated chapel windows looking down from the first floor, is of a theatrical elegance, while the main rooms of the castle are spacious and lofty, those on the west side framing fine views of the ruined fortress of Beaucaire just opposite across the Rhône. By clambering up to the battlements of the castle, while the wind tears at your hair, you can gaze downwards at the turbid waters of the river, or out across the huddled roof-tops of the town of Tarascon to the vineyards, and the bare hills and pale mountains of Provence. This huge but compact building, guarding the crossing of the Rhône, gives one a far more valid sense of medieval Provence than all the vaunted debris of Les Baux.

René of Anjou, nominal king of Sicily, who completed the castle of Tarascon, and used it as an alternative residence to his palace of Aix (long since destroyed), was the last real sovereign of an independent Provence; for his heir and nephew, Charles du Maine, dying shortly after he had succeeded his uncle, bequeathed the county of Provence to the French crown in 1481. Provence had come to the house of Anjou in 1246, by the marriage of a daughter of Raymond-Béranger IV, Count of Toulouse, with the brother of King Louis IX of France: and, though the Arelate or kingdom of Arles* was still nominally the property of the Holy Roman Empire, the princes of two successive houses of Anjou claimed and ruled it, taking part in the civil wars which ravaged this southern countryside, and leading Provençal armies into Italy for their various Neapolitan campaigns. For Provence, the importance of René of Anjou lay in his role as a civilized Renaissance prince, a patron of painters and poets in his courts of Aix and Tarascon, and ruling the country with mildness and a pious benevolence, rather than with brilliance, energy or statecraft. Like that of Marius, the memory of King René still hovers over Provence,

*In AD 418 the capital of Roman Gaul had been moved southwards from Trèves, rendered untenable by barbarian incursions, to Arles. During the Dark Ages the territory now known as Provence was occupied by various invaders from the north – Visigoths, Ostrogoths and Lotharingians – and also ravaged by the Saracens in the ninth and tenth centuries. The territory became incorporated in the *regnum Burgundiae*, and in the twelfth century the expression 'kingdom of Arles' is first used. In 1032 succession to the kingdom fell to the Emperor Henry II on the death of Rodolph III of Burgundy. The very obscure history of this kingdom from that period to the end of the fifteenth century is well elucidated by Professor Paul Fournier in Chapter IX of the *Cambridge Medieval History*, volume 8 (Cambridge University Press, 1936).

and he too has become a figure of legend, and in some senses a byword. In the days of the Abbé Papon, the learned Oratorian whose *Histoire générale de Provence*, published not long before the French Revolution, has remained one of the most reliable as well as one of the most readable works upon its subject,* the people of Marseilles would repeat that King René's favourite pastime was to walk, simply and unattended, along the quayside of their port on sunny days, and from this memory the people of the country still called any sun-warmed nook '*la Cheminée du Roi René*'. René's actual appearance may best be judged from his kneeling portrait on the left wing of the triptych of the *Buisson Ardent* in the Cathedral of Aix, while his statue by David d'Angers at the head of the Cours Mirabeau in that city epitomizes the benign, romantic figure of popular myth. In the king's hand the sculptor has placed a bunch of muscat grapes, for to René is attributed the introduction of this fruit into Provence, as well as that of carnations, roses and peacocks, and the encouragement of the allied industries of mulberry-growing and the breeding of silk-worms. The king himself illuminated, and wrote poems and treatises. He was also, say the Provençaux, a great lover: for to the good King René are posthumously attributed all those qualities which the people of his country most admire.

Whatever attributes this cultivated prince may or may not have possessed, there is no question of his profound piety. He instigated the performance of miracle plays throughout his Angevin and Provençal dominions, and much embellished the churches of Tarascon and other towns. In 1448, at his orders, a meticulous investigation was carried out beneath the remote fortress-church of the Saintes-Maries-de-la-Mer in the Camargue. The object of this search, of which the official contemporary account survives today, was to find the relics of the two Maries – Marie Jacobé and Marie Salomé – who are said to have landed on that desolate shore in AD 40, in flight from persecution in Judaea, accompanied by Mary Magdalen, Maximin, Lazarus, and Sarah, a black serving-maid. Marie Jacobé and Marie Salomé, with Sarah, are alleged to have

---

*Histoire générale de Provence par M. l-Abbé Papon, de l'Académie de Marseille (Paris, 1777–86, four volumes). J.F. Papon (1734–1803) spent many years of research amongst the archives of the cities and monastic establishments of Provence and produced a work of lasting value.

remained where they had landed, building an oratory on the site of a pagan temple, while the others dispersed eastwards to Marseilles, to Aix and to the cave in the Sainte-Baume. Since the seventeenth century, the authenticity of King René's finds has been questioned, but, as Lenthéric has shown in an impartial and exhaustive survey of all the evidence, there is no more reason to disbelieve the traditional legend than there is to believe it. This story of the first Christianization of Gaul has been disputed. It has never been disproved.

IV

The road from Arles to Les-Saintes-Maries-de-la-Mer leads straight across the sandy flats of the Camargue, a waste, salt land tufted with coarse, spiky grasses, and intersected by shallow streamlets and canals. Here and there on the white and shimmering horizon crouches the dark shape of an old *mas* with wind-bent trees before it, and sometimes you pass a cluster of cabins about a lonely church. As you drive out in a seaward direction on this plain you become slowly aware that waiting for you in the distance, by the shore, is a stranger silhouette than any of these. It might, at first sight, be a giant windmill, or a stranded galleon, or a castle tower, or an embattled gateway leading to no town. Then suddenly you realize that this must be the church of the Saintes-Maries.

The fortified church of the Saintes-Maries-de-la-Mer was built in the twelfth century on what was believed to be the remains of an oratory constructed for Marie Jacobé, sister of the Virgin Mary, and Marie Salomé, the mother of James and John. As Lenthéric has made clear,* there is nothing intrinsically impossible, nor even unlikely, in the traditional tale that a handful of notable refugees from religious persecution on the eastern seaboard of the Mediterranean should have escaped in a ship bound for one of the Greek cities of Provence – ports which maintained a thriving oriental trade – and should have landed by accident or by design at a fishing village on the coast near

*Charles Lenthéric, the author of a number of important books of scholarship on the early history and archaeology of Provence, deals fully with the question of the Saintes-Maries legends in the second volume of his great work, *Le Rhône, histoire d'un fleuve* (Plon, Paris, 1892, two volumes).

Arles. Archaeological discoveries in the hamlet of the Saintes-Maries testify to the existence on this shore in the first century AD of a fishing community which spoke Latin and venerated Roman and Greek gods. One such piece of evidence was in fact turned up during the investigations of 1448, although the experts employed by King René did not correctly interpret what they found. Searching for the bodies of the two Maries who were traditionally supposed to have been buried underneath the fortress church, these fifteenth-century archaeologists unearthed a marble slab bearing the mystifying, and indeed incomprehensible, word AVAC. The contemporary record of these investigations relates that, after much bewilderment, the scholars produced an ingenious theory of what these letters spelled: it was the Latin word CAVA, or vault, written backwards and was thus taken as a cryptic direction on where to dig. Some bones were soon found, and these King René placed in a new chapel built for the purpose over the apse of the church: here the relics remain, and they are ceremoniously lowered on a pulley wreathed with flowers during the fêtes of May and of October every year. In the course of time the marble slab with its odd inscription has disappeared. It became easy for sceptical archaeologists to declare that this stone had never existed, and that the record of it was nothing but a pious medieval fraud, equivalent to the 'discovery' of the body of the Magdalen by the monks of Vézelay in the eleventh century, and casting doubt on the good faith of King René and on the whole story of the relics at Les Saintes-Maries. But one of the chief nineteenth-century opponents of the legend, Otto Hirschfeld, who compiled a monumental catalogue of the Latin inscriptions of Gallia Narbonensis published in Berlin in 1888, had just listed this inscription amongst those which were palpably false, when he discovered, in the libraries of the Vatican and of Carpentras, two further accounts of the marble of Les Saintes-Maries. Both of these were by reliable travellers neither of whom had any interest in the cult of the Saintes-Maries, both were of the sixteenth century, both showed that the stone not only existed, but had survived until their day. And one of these accounts quite clearly proved that what the inexperienced scholars of King René had hopefully interpreted as CAVA written backwards was in fact part of a Roman dedication to 'august goddesses' and really read 'AVG'.

Whether the relics in the chapel over the apse be genuine or not, there is a quality of the marvellous about the church of the Saintes-Maries, a holy fortress on the very edge of the Mediterranean, behind it the melancholy wilderness of the Camargue and ahead of it the stony beaches and the restless sea. A small village of fisher-people's houses surrounds the church. There are commonplace villas on the sea-front, and some large modern cafés capable of accommodating the swarms of pilgrims who go there twice a year. In the crypt of the church is the untidy shrine of the black servant Sarah, who receives the gipsies' homage every year – a place frowsty with old clothing and black with candle-grease. The church above it is a splendid example of those Romanesque buildings, half church, half strong-hold, which the memory of the Saracen invasions, and the hazards of daily life in the eleventh and twelfth centuries, made necessary to a small community in a place as isolated as Les Saintes-Maries. Even when one has seen it two or three times, this church seems equally mysterious: indeed the more you visit it, the more wonderful it will become. By a combined effect of its architecture, its situation, and the ancient Christian traditions associated with it, the church of the Saintes-Maries-de-la-Mer seizes not only on the imagination but on the heart and the affections. It is with a sense of sharp regret that one leaves to go back to Arles, across the desolate Camargue in the gathering evening light.

V

The main structure of the church of the Saintes-Maries is thought to have been built between the years 1140 and 1180. Towards the end of the same century, the legend of the Christianization of the Rhône delta by the immediate disciples of Christ received further public confirmation when, in 1187, the ecclesiastical authorities of Tarascon announced that they had discovered a sarcophagus containing the true body of Martha, sister of Mary and hostess of Christ. That Martha's body lay at Tarascon had been common knowledge in the Rhône valley for many generations, but the timing of this official declaration is significant, for it came at a moment when general European interest in the whereabouts of these saints' relics was at its height. The church at Les-Saintes-Maries was being built; the monks of Vézelay announced that they possessed the body of the Magdalen, brought, so they said, northward from Provence to Burgundy at the time of the Saracen invasions; and even in remote England the same epoch saw the Somerset legend of Joseph of Arimathea at Glastonbury taking shape. In each of these cases – Les-Saintes-Maries, Vézelay, Glastonbury – the churches concerned became centres of important pilgrimages, bringing rich offerings for the saints' shrines and business to the towns which owned them. Tarascon was no exception, and it was recognized as one of the most thriving places of pilgrimage in all Provence.

The story of Saint Martha and the Tarasque – a dragon from whose ravages she saved the peoples of the delta, by subduing the beast and persuading it to plunge into the Rhône – is familiar to everyone who has been in Provence. Representations of the Saint and the Tarasque – that on a fifteenth-century side altar in Aix cathedral, for instance – are frequently seen in Provençal churches, and the ebullient festival of the Tarasque, instituted by the good King René, is still celebrated at Tarascon. It is evident that the tale of Saint Martha and the dragon originated in some natural confusion between the Martha of the Gospels and Martha the Syrian prophetess whom Plutarch describes as accompanying Marius' armies in a litter during the victorious Provençal campaign of 102 BC, and whom he says that the Roman general consulted before any engagement of arms. Like her protector, this Syrian Martha – who did in fact contribute to save the delta people from the ravages of the barbarians – lives on in the folk-memory of Provence, and it is easy to see that in the course of time she has become transformed and Christianized by identification with the sister of Mary. A new church, consecrated in 1197, was raised over the 'relics' of Saint Martha: much enlarged in the fourteenth century, this church was desecrated during the French Revolution, and almost demolished by American bombers attacking the nearby Rhône bridge in 1944. The tympanum and portal of the church of Saint Martha once bore fine Romanesque sculptures perhaps equal in quality to those of Sainte-Trophime at Arles, but these were defaced in the Revolution, while in 1944 the tower, and large portions of the body of the church, were blown away. Deep in a crypt in the foundations of the old church, the tomb of Saint Martha remains intact. It contains one of the most remarkable tomb figures in any church in Provence.

To reach the crypt, you pass through the cold and rubbly nave of the bombed building, and descend a broad first flight of stairs. This takes you on to a species of mezzanine or landing just below ground level, where stands the fine Renaissance tomb of the seneschal of King René. Another staircase, narrower and more shadowy, leads down at right angles into the twilit crypt. On entering this small crypt you feel that you are alone in the darkness, and then you become slowly aware of the silent presence of a great immobile figure, a recumbent corpse with feet pointing towards the staircase and hands folded on its breast. If you light the candles held in iron sconces round this effigy, you find yourself gazing down on the realistic marble face of a dead nun, who is shown clad in wimple and conventual robes, her eyes closed, her face expressionless and smooth. This uncanny marble effigy, propped rather than laid upon a sumptuous marble *lit de parade*, is of Genoese origin, and was commissioned by an Italian Archbishop of Avignon in the middle of the seventeenth century; the tomb below it houses the fifth-century sarcophagus in which the alleged relics of the saint were disinterred. To find this spectacular *seicento* monument upon the western threshold of Provence is unexpected, but to the traveller on his first journey to the country it can seem symbolic: for here, on the high road to Avignon, the little arcaded river town of Tarascon provides this concrete evidence of the pervasive Italianizing influence which spread outward from the papal city in the sixteenth, seventeenth and eighteenth centuries, tingeing this corner of Provence with Italy. Moreover, the legendary activities of Saint Martha in the Rhône valley concern Avignon also, for she was long reverenced as the founder of the chief church in that city, Notre-Dame-des-Doms. For these reasons, as well as for the mysterious allure of this tomb-figure in itself, a stranger will do well to pause at Tarascon, penetrate into the crypt, and gaze at the serene effigy lying there in the lemon-yellow light of the wax candles, which casts its noble silhouette, fluttering and magnified, over the crypt's low ceiling. Emerging into the upper air and beside the windy Rhône, he may then pass on his way through fields and vineyards sheltered by cypress screens to Avignon's stiff ramparts and crenellated walls. He should aim to enter Avignon at nightfall.

CHAPTER SEVEN

I

IDEALLY AVIGNON SHOULD BE approached by water, but for travellers today this immemorial manner of entering the city – stepping ashore in the sunlight when the boat has glided up to the hot quayside – is no longer possible. The few steamers that still ply up and down the Rhône do not take passengers. A first glimpse of Avignon from up-river has often been described – by Mérimée and by Mistral and by Dickens in particular. To boats bearing down from the Pont Saint-Esprit, the sudden twist of the Rhône revealed the arches of the famous old bridge, snapped and stranded in midstream. On the one hand spread the leafy banks of the island of La Barthelasse (with here and there the painted trellis-work of summer restaurants), on the other the shadowless pale walls of Avignon stood back from the water's edge. Behind and above these walls the rigid structure of the Palace of the Popes loomed over billowing housetops, tiled in red. Beside it rose the hill, then crowned by crooked windmills, now a tidy *jardin anglais*, called 'le Rocher des Doms'. To land at Avignon emphasized the major fact about this strong walled city: its relationship to the Rhône. Today this connection is most clearly seen from the cramped window of an aeroplane. You peer down upon a rhomboid town set in a landscape like crumpled brown paper, sheltered in a fold of the Rhône and safely ringed by walls.

The walls of Avignon are the dominant feature of the city if you approach it by road, or from the railway station, well placed upon a knoll beyond the limits of the town. There is a palpable sense of excitement about entering a walled city after sundown which it is hard to analyse. It is a sense both of protection and expectancy. You feel it as you come into Aigues-Mortes towards evening, or when, returning into Siena on a summer night after a walk through the moonlit Tuscan countryside, you pass beneath one of the lofty, deep arched gateways of the city, with the tall wooden doors battened back. To enter Avignon at nightfall by the Porte de la République can seem too good to be true. This grave, authentic-looking gateway, with its tidy *mâchicoulis* and incisive crenellations, is at first sight fantastically romantic. On a second look, by daylight, it appears a shade self-conscious and theatrical. You wonder, and then suspect the truth; for, like much of the surviving wall of Avignon, this gateway with its neat twin towers is the creation of the nineteenth-century architect, Eugène Emmanuel Viollet-le-Duc, and like Carcassonne or the massive, gloomy Château de Pierrefonds, it forms a good example of those architectural processes by which the age of Louis-Philippe and Napoleon III sought to repair the double ravages of time and of the French Revolution upon the monuments of France. 'The term Restoration and the thing itself are both modern,' wrote Viollet-le-Duc. 'To restore a building is not to preserve it, to repair or rebuild it, it is to reinstate it in a condition of completeness which could never have existed at any given time . . . and, in fact, no civilization, no people of bygone ages, has conceived the idea of making restorations in the sense in which we comprehend them.'* It was in strong adherence to these precepts that Viollet-le-Duc directed work upon the crumbling walls and ramparts of Avignon – repointing them, rebacking them, renewing *mâchicoulis* galleries, piercing fresh gateways, and in general furbishing-up what wars had left of the great system of moated defence works thrown round the city in the reign of the fourteenth-century Pope, Clement V.

It is now fashionable to decry Viollet-le-Duc, and to make fun of his school of restoration. Their ideas seem to us preposterous, their achievements elegant fakes. Yet in fact the theory of total rehabilitation for some decrepit building was a sober and honest attempt to solve the eternal problem which faces all archaeologists as well as all historical and biographical writers, and which confronts the traveller and tourist constantly. This is the problem of feeling one's way backwards into time, and reaching some sense of intimacy with a vanished epoch. In other words it is the problem of believing in the past, of convincing oneself that it ever did really exist.

Neither the caverns of Les Baux nor the shallow entrenchments

---

*On Restoration, translated with a notice of Viollet-le-Duc's works by C. Wethered (London 1875). This is a separate issue of the article on Restoration from Viollet-le-Duc's *Dictionnaire raisonnée de l'architecture française* (1858–68).

and fine monuments of Glanum can persuade us that these derelict sites were once vigorous and animated places. With Avignon the case is different. Here we are living in a city which, despite the ravages of the Revolution, is still largely intact. Moreover, in its heyday Avignon was not just a wealthy southern city, but one of the most important and powerful cities in Europe. When the Papacy (already owner of the Comtat Venaissin) moved to Avignon from Rome in 1309, the focal point of the Christian world shifted from the banks of the Tiber to those of the Rhône. Finally purchased by the Pope from Joanna of Naples in 1348, Avignon became an international centre of luxury and learning. Crowded to overflowing, too small to cope adequately with the first influx of the cardinals of the papal court, the city was enlarged and embellished, becoming a byword for extravagance and show. After the decisive return of the papacy to Rome in 1403, Avignon was governed by papal legates, but it remained a rich cosmopolitan city, for centuries the refuge of those fleeing from French and Italian justice, as well as for English religious and political exiles. Modern Avignon is beautiful, gay and lively; but along its ramparts, in its side-streets lined by small *palazzos*, churches and penitents' chapels, above all in the great empty halls and stairways of the castle of the popes, we are haunted by a perpetual doubt. It is the same doubt that assails us beside the slate-grey canals of Bruges, a city formerly so ostentatious and splendid, now moribund and picturesque, or on the wide sunlit *piazza* of Urbino before that ducal palace, once one of the marvels of Renaissance Europe, now silent and deserted. Faced by the vacant monuments of the past, by bleak council chambers bare of hangings, by weed-grown courtyards in which horses used to rear and trample, by private chapels with floors that knees have worn away, the act of faith in the past becomes more, not less, difficult. How are we to believe that these places were ever other than we see them today, chilling and lifeless, echoing only to the guide's monologue and the tourists' shuffling feet? Standing in the *salle de l'audience* of the palace at Avignon, it is as hard to believe that the Popes and their legates held court here, as it is to persuade oneself that the tranquil plateau of wild flowers and grass near Saint-Rémy was once the thriving market-place of Roman Glanum. The past is one of the many things in life we take on trust.

II

Apart from straining our credulity, the Palace of the Popes suffers (in common with most other monuments open to the public) from the added disadvantage of being shown by a loquacious guide to persons in groups. At Saint-Rémy you can wander alone and at will through the garden of Saint-Paul-du-Mausolée. In Maillane the villa of Mistral is usually empty. At Les Baux always, and in the Arles amphitheatre sometimes, it is possible to escape from other tourists. But in the papal palace, as in the châteaux of the Loire, you are one of a flock. Supplying the human equation needed to bring out the scale of the vast, high-vaulted chambers of this palace, one's fellow-travellers do this in a manner at once inadequate and obtrusive; for as they clamber panting up a spiral staircase or trot beneath a Gothic arch, you find that their personalities force themselves on your attention, until you are no longer looking at the building through which you are drifting, but are watching and listening to them instead. Those avid-looking girls with cameras must be Americans, you think; that handsome boy in shorts is Swiss. How offensive that anyone should be quite that ugly; whatever can it mean? I don't know if this distracting curiosity about stray people is general, or peculiar; I have certainly found it, over and over again, most detrimental to a clear impression of some place or building, and I need hardly add, to the search for the past. Sightseeing should be done alone, or in the company of one silent, sensitive, humorous and well-instructed companion. But there are very few things in life one is allowed to do alone. Visiting the Palace of the Popes is not among them.

To gain the palace you must cross a wide, commercial-looking square, at present called Place Georges-Clemenceau. This square, large and dreary, and containing a number of big cafés, is perhaps the only ugly and unsympathetic part of Avignon. Pass swiftly through it, turn diagonally to the right, and you will reach the cobbled Place du Palais, fronting on which the papal palace stands.

Each time you see it, the Palace of the Popes impresses you by its severity and strength. It looks noble. It looks independent and self-contained. The apparent simplicity of this huge building is reinforced by two nearby contrasts – the ornate façade of the papal mint opposite the palace, decorated by stone swags of fruit so bulky that they seem designed for some larger edifice, and the giant nineteenth-century figure of the Virgin which caps the tower of the church of Notre-Dame-des-Doms. These neighbours to the palace, the one so elaborate, the other so sentimental, accentuate its essentially functional quality; for though Mérimée was exaggerating when he described the papal palace as more like the citadel of some Asiatic tyrant than the home of the Vicar of the God of Peace, this massive building has the aspect of a powerful fortress. It was, in fact, designed primarily for defence.

The first French pope to settle at Avignon, Clement V, moved thither in 1309. He did no building. Always expecting to return to Rome, he spent the years of his pontificate as the guest of the Dominicans in a monastery beside the Rhône. His successor John XXII set up court in the episcopal palace of Avignon, next to the cathedral, and it was this palace which was transformed by the next two popes into the vast castle which we see today. Benedict XII constructed the Old Palace, on the side of the Rocher des Doms; on to this Clement VI tacked the New Palace, dominating the town. The haste with which this great mass of buildings was thrown up – both palaces were completed in a space of twenty years – accounts no doubt for the cumbrousness and lack of symmetry and unity of the whole: 'a true chaos, a body without a soul', a French writer of the Renaissance period called it, a confused building lacking every architectural merit, erected neither for pleasure nor for comfort. This judgement of a contemporary of the men who created Fontainebleau and Bois, Chenonceaux and Azay-le-Rideau, is however unduly harsh, for the interior of the Papal palace was decorated and furnished with the greatest splendour, painters and sculptors from all over Europe being employed upon the task. All that now remains of their sumptuous embellishments are the worn frescos by Sienese painters in the two chapels of Saint Martial and Saint John, the lovely pastoral scenes discovered in the present century upon the walls of a chamber in the Tour de la Garde Robe, and a string of faded prophets against a bright blue ground powdered with golden stars which has survived in one small section of the vaulted ceiling of the Salle de la Grande Audience.

La Salle de la Grande Audience is the first important room shown you when, having penetrated within the palace walls and crossed the rough courtyard, you are shepherded through a dark guard-room containing a Madonna by Mignard and agreeably decorated with martial trophies painted in seventeenth-century grisaille. Here in the audience chamber, where the courts of the successive pontiffs, and later, of their legates, were at their most hieratic and most splendid, with dignitaries and their attendants in murmurous throngs, with vivid tapestries and alabaster thrones, there now broods a sense of space and stark mortality. Two ranks of clustering pillars support a great extent of cold stone vaulting above a great expanse of cold stone floor. The surviving prophets glimmer like wraiths against their gold-and-blue background. Allowed to decay during the long nineteenth-century occupation of the palace as a military barracks, some of these frescos were also deliberately mutilated by the soldiers, who, knowing that they could sell frag-ments of the paintings to curious travellers, devised a special kind of knife to peel the profitable figures from the stone. At one end of the audience chamber a shallow staircase of rounded, flowing steps, like tidemarks on wet sand, leads gently upwards, conducting one to the private apartments of the palace, and to the rooms actually inhabited by the fourteenth-century popes.

All great castles and palaces of the past contain at least one set of rooms – often enough small and low-ceilinged – in which the princes who owned them really lived, sheltered from the pompous official life of the public apartments. These private suites were usually the most exquisitely ornamented, and it is these, and not the vast rooms built for state and show, that give you a sense of intimacy and of actual life. These are the rooms one prefers most and remembers longest – the little rooms of Isabella d'Este at Mantua, for example, with cupboards for her music and her books; the inlaid study of Federigo da Montefeltro at Urbino; the gilded library of the Grand Duke Cosimo in the Signoria; the oratory of Anne de Bretagne at Loches; the panelled rooms of Cardinal Wolsey overlooking the sunny Pond Garden of Hampton Court. In the frescoed rooms of the Wardrobe Tower, and in the papal bedchamber, we find at Avignon, in a dilapidated and indeed skeletal condition, the equivalents of these.

The 'profane' murals of the room in the Wardrobe Tower, vaguely attributed to the 'School of Avignon' (a local studio, seemingly under Sienese direction), show a series of elegant pastoral scenes – fishing, hunting, bird-snaring, bathing in a pool. The scenes are laid in a countryside of poetical and formal beauty – feathery trees with slender trunks and blue-green leaves grow amidst hummocks of flowered grass, while in the background is an undergrowth of close, trim foliage, thickets of wild briar, ferns and white hawthorn. This landscape, carried round all four walls, must once have given the illusion of stepping into an enchanted wood. The persons and the animals who inhabit these scenes look tranquilly preoccupied, and seem to be living happily within the dimensions of their painted paradise. A white hound lollops forward over the grass tufts, a man with a net fishes in an oblong stone-edged pond beside which three more people sit or stand. In another place a youth stretches upwards to a fruit tree, in another a man with a hunting-spear in his hand stands talking to a child. The condition of all these frescos is poor and frayed, but the illusion of beauty which they convey is not. In the papal bedchamber above this room all that remains of the decorations are some hanging bird-cages painted on the walls near the windows, and shown as holding captive bright blue and yellow birds. From a window in this bedchamber may be gained one of the most authentic views of Avignon – for you look down across the faded orange roof-tops of the city, their tiles seeming as soft and tangled as loosely knitted wool, with here and there an upright church tower, or the lime-green patch of a square shaded by trees. This view gives you an indelible impression of the hot, seething vitality of the old town baking there in the sunlight, all the more sensible in contrast to the cold empty rooms through which one has been led.

The tour of the papal palace, best done guidebook in hand, is a long and often an exhausting process. Footsore, and blinking in the sunlight, you emerge into the streets of Avignon supported by the sense of fulfilment and also of relief which many conscientious sightseers must feel: for, implicit in the fascination of this most delightful of activities lies its corollary – the elation of escape from the tyranny of the sights we ought to see. How many of us have not felt a certain sneaking satisfaction, towards the end of a long day of sightseeing, at finding the penultimate chapel, or the final museum, firmly, irrevocably, shut?

A first visit to the papal palace over, and after a rest and a drink.

one may then begin the most exciting part of a stay in Avignon – the gradual exploration of its streets. Here in steep lanes where women lean fron window-ledges talking, where children scuffle round a bicycle, or an old lady snatches up a cat to kiss, you find doorways and whole façades of extraordinary beauty, carved details unrecorded in the guides. Avignon is a superlative example of a city which repays casual and random exploration – as much as Aix-en-Provence, far more than Arles. There are the crossing branches carved in stone, as delicate as stags' antlers, above the entrance to the fifteenth-century Palais du Rouve; the seventeenth-century windows of the Hôtel Crillon; the provincial gilded woodwork of the Chapelle des Pénitents Noirs; the marble relief of Christ carrying the Cross by Francesco Laurana in the church of Saint-Didier; the porch and steps of Saint-Agricole; the stone sunrise upon the portico of the eighteenth-century theatre near the Hôtel de l'Europe and the Porte de l'Oulle.

In general the churches and monastic buildings of Avignon were stripped of their contents during the Revolution. In 1892 what was left of these spoils – pictures, sculpture, books, manuscripts – was gathered together and housed in a municipal museum. Thirty years later these collections were merged with those left to the town of Avignon by a Doctor Calvet, and today, enriched by certain subsequent bequests, they form part of one of the most agreeable provincial museums to be seen anywhere in France – the famous Musée Calvet, established since 1835 in the lovely Louis Quinze Hôtel de Villeneuve-Martignan. This well-arranged and elegant museum perfectly illustrates the history of the arts in Avignon. A series of visits to it should be regarded as an essential factor of any stay in that town.

III

After the stuffy, overloaded museums of Arles and Aix, the Musée Calvet does not at first seem like a museum at all. The hôtel which the Comte de Villeneuve commissioned from the architect Franque in 1741, and which was completed fourteen years later, still bears the aspect of a private residence, with iron gates protecting a wide courtyard, a chain of ground-floor rooms of which the original panelling and chimneypieces still happily survive, and a quiet garden where urns and statues gleam beneath dark trees. 'In this place,' wrote Stendhal of the garden of the Musée Calvet, 'reigns a profound tranquillity reminding me of the beautiful churches of Italy; a soul already partly freed from the vain interests of the world is here disposed to apprehend the beauty of the sublime.' Peaceful and unexacting, the benign atmosphere of this most charming museum does in fact tempt one to return. Its contents are varied, and these inevitably include a mass of Roman and Gallo-Roman fragments, more interesting to the student than to the casual visitor. The museum has also certain good objects and works of art – a fifteenth-century *Adoration* by an unknown Avignonnese painter; a severe, compassionate portrait of an aged nun by Louis Lenain; a smiling head of a boy in white marble attributed to Desiderio da Settignano; the ivory Christ made by Guillermin in 1659 for the Confraternity of the Pénitents Noirs of Avignon; David's *Death of Bara*; a good Corot of Italy; and so on. But apart from these the chief interest of this museum lies in its demonstration of the extraordinary richness of the church establishments of Avignon before the French Revolution. Conversely, in the pathetic debris of the great fourteenth- and fifteenth-century tombs which once ornamented every church in Avignon, we gain too a clear idea of the peculiar violence of the Revolution in Provence.

If these broken tombs of the Musée Calvet – in particular those of Urban V and the Cardinal de Lagrange – testify to the magnificence of medieval Avignon, and to the ferocity of the Provençal revolutionaries, some of them demonstrate almost equally the disastrous restoring zeal of local antiquaries in the last century. The most notable example of this is not to be seen in the museum, however, but in the cathedral church of Notre-Dame-des-Doms, where the lofty canopied tomb of Pope John XXII, completed in 1345 and hacked to pieces in 1789, was patched together again in the reign of Louis Philippe, when, the original effigy being lost, the recumbent figure of some unknown bishop was interpolated. In happy contrast to the faked effect of this misguided restoration is the other important Avignonnese papal tomb surviving from this epoch – the marvellous memorial to Innocent VI, erected in 1362 in the Chartreuse du Val-de-Bénédiction at Villeneuve-lès-Avignon, and today preserved in the chapel of the hospital of that beautiful village. With the exception of the effigy in white marble, this tomb is entirely constructed in Pernes stone. It is shown you from a gallery in the chapel by an old nun wearing a winged headdress tilted forward over her eyes. In its tapering grace and ethereal lightness the tomb reminds one of the finest of those gothic tombs which have survived the English Reformation – Tewkesbury, or Winchester, or the half-ruined effigies of Westminster. But it is a scene very different from Winchester cloisters or Tewkesbury close that faces you as you follow the old nun out of the chapel, down the stone stairs and through an arch beyond which the old men and women of the hospice are sitting under the plane trees, sheltered from the blazing sun. The narrow hot white street of Villeneuve, lined on one side by cool arcades, seems to epitomize one aspect of Provence. Separated from Avignon by the two branches of the Rhône and the island of la Barthelasse, Villeneuve is at once calmer and more restful than that city. It is also the home – one is tempted to say the shrine – of a fine fourteenth-century ivory statue, the celebrated *vierge d'ivoire*, which is kept in a safe in the sacristy of the chief church of Villeneuve-lès-Avignon, dedicated to Our Lady and founded by Pope John XXII's nephew in 1333.

IV

Seen from the Porte de l'Oulle at Avignon by the early morning or the evening light, the low-lying panorama of Villeneuve, less than two miles away across the water, shines with all the soft poetic glow which Corot saw and painted. By the glare of midday the gritty white road over the suspension bridge, and the tall tower built into the rock upon the farther shore, stand out too starkly; the prospect of leaving the shelter of the gate, or the shadow of the plane trees along the nearby bank, is more intimidating; but, then, who goes anywhere at midday in Provence? As you drive across the Rhône towards Villeneuve at nightfall, the view disintegrates into its components, and becomes itemized, and thus historical – in the foreground the tower of Philippe le Bel, which that French monarch built upon a rock to dominate the foreign territory of Avignon in 1302, and behind it, to northward, the pale winding walls of the Fort Saint-André, a vast fortification erected sixty years later to protect the Benedictine monastery of that name, and which, enclosing this and its village in one great military installation, further strengthened the French strongpoint at the tower. The fortifications of Saint-André look sluggish and swollen. Between the tower and the fort lurk the roof-tops of Villeneuve, above which rises the big Gothic church of Our Lady, supported down its length by flying buttresses, at its west end a tower as military-looking as any castle keep, at its eastern end two fiercely pointed pinnacles.

Once over the river, you can look at Avignon, the view of which from certain points along this road is without equal. It was at one of these points that we stopped for a few moments on the first evening that I ever went to Villeneuve, and in recollection of this incident I have always paused there since. I was travelling with a French friend of mine and with his mother. It was she who suggested the halt. 'I should like to stop here,' she said, 'for this is the best view of Avignon of all; and I have reached an age when I realize that I may be doing something for the last time. In all probability I shall never see Avignon again.' Pausing there since, I have sometimes thought how this is what we should all, at any age, feel about a given place, and wondered why it seems impossible to suppose that one may never see, say, Avignon again. And yet a sense of the transitoriness of human life gives an added tang to the manifold pleasures of existence, and can even come to seem itself a separate source of happiness.

When we reached the centre of Villeneuve, that same evening, it seemed strangely quiet after Avignon, and somehow small-scale and compact. The tiny square beside the buttressed church wall has some plane trees, and the street leading from it towards the hospice has arcades. The church cast a long shadow on the earth road. There was no one about but a stout, reliable-looking old curé in a black biretta, his full-skirted black cassock bound in by a wide black silk-fringed sash. He was reading his office from a small black prayer-book as he paced up and down before the church in the rays of the sinking sun. Presently a little boy in a yellow jersey appeared round the corner of the church, bouncing, in a maddeningly incompetent manner, an orange rubber ball. There are few noises in this world more insidious and more irritating than the sound of a child bouncing a rubber ball.

Inside, the church was dark and cool, and smelt of musty incense. Along the nave, shallow side-chapels were made sombre by those vast, dim, high-slung, badly varnished canvases of the seventeenth century to be seen in every big provincial church in France. The main altar, a complicated baroque construction of 1745 with heavy pillars, angels in obeisance and a crucifix on a marble rock, has a fine relief, also in marble, of Christ entombed and was made for the chapel of the Chartreuse du Val-de-Bénédiction, founded by Innocent VI on the site of his summer palace, and now a desecrated establishment with a splendid Renaissance gateway opening off the long main street of Villeneuve. To the left of the altar is the door of the sacristy – a small gloomy room added to the church in the fifteenth century – in which the ivory Virgin lives; but in spite of constantly ringing the bell near it for the sacristan, no one appeared. Such difficulties, and the waiting they involve, give force to one's determination and edge to one's desire; after ten minutes' more fruitless tugging at the bell-rope, we appealed to the old priest outside the church, who genially arranged to have the door unlocked. We were ushered into the sacristy. The steel safe in which the figure is kept swung open, and rather surprisingly revealed a smart glass showcase lined with velvet, and as brightly illuminated as anything in the most up-to-date museum. Inside the showcase, on a turn-table which revolves slowly at the pressure of a button, stands the ivory statuette, coloured in polychrome, of the crowned Virgin and Child, one of the superlative achievements of sculpture in early fourteenth-century France. The figure has a lilting stance, an insouciant elegance, and on its face a light and serene smile. Also in the sacristy is a marble Janus-faced Virgin and Child, also of the fourteenth century; this figure, facing both ways, is squatter, jollier and somehow more plebeian than the ivory figure. By the time we were ready to leave the church dusk was closing in on Villeneuve. As we left the old priest showed us the little derelict cloister of the church, reached from the street through an arch in the east wall. In the middle of this deserted cloister two graceful elder trees are growing from the bare untended earth.

Villeneuve-lès-Avignon is also known as the place of origin of two great religious pictures of fifteenth-century Provence – the Villeneuve *Pietà* by an unknown painter, now in the Louvre, and the *Coronation of the Virgin*, painted in 1542 by Charenton, and still preserved in Villeneuve. While both rank as products of the 'School of Avignon', in neither case is this term indubitably correct. Even after the return of the papacy to Rome the court of Avignon continued to attract painters from many parts of Europe, and it has been considered that the Villeneuve *Pietà* is in fact the work of a Catalan artist,* while the painter of the *Coronation*, Enguerrand Charenton, born at Laon, was one of several exponents of the Flemish Gothic style employed in fifteenth-century Avignon. This *Coronation*, an *Entombment* by Simon de Chalons containing a portrait of Innocent VI, a modern copy of the *Pietà*, and certain other pictures including a *Crucifixion* by Philippe de Champaigne are now exhibited, like the Memlincs at Bruges, in a room of the hospital of Villeneuve. This room, and its ante-chamber, and the great staircase of the fine seventeenth-century hôtel in which the hospital is lodged, are shown by the same old nun who conducts one into the hospital chapel to see the tomb of Innocent VI, and who seems as crippled and as aged as the octogenarians for whom she and the other members of her order care. This atmosphere of quiet old age well suits the tranquil streets of Villeneuve. It has often seemed to me that in Provence, as in Italy, the decline of life comes more naturally than in England or some other northern place. Age seems to lose its horrors in this red-soiled country, where the gnarled olive trees look as ancient as the Roman amphitheatres, and almost every hamlet has some monument of the remote past standing near it, ruined and crumbling in the hot sun and the driving wind. As one wanders through the Provençal villages there is nothing shocking or unreal in the reflection that these old wrinkled women in black shawls, these crabbed old men hobbling with a stick, were once as lithe and young as the quick dark youths and girls with glistening hair and skin whose laughter rings along the streets and

---

*The Catalan origin of the *Pietà*, accepted by M. Vaudoyer in his recent work, *La Peinture provençale* (Paris, 1949), is, however, rejected by Dr Grete Ring in her far more scholarly *A Century of French Painting*, *1400–1500* (Phaidon Press, 1949). Here, after marshalling all the evidence, Dr Ring declares it her opinion that 'the picture is the work of a Provençal master who has not yet been identified, and to whom no other picture could be attributed until now'.

through the vineyard fields. There is an immemorial, and thus an inevitable, quality about the course of human living in Provence.

V

It was on this first visit to Avignon that I made the mistake, never since repeated, of going to see the Fountain of Petrarch at Vaucluse. This legendary fountain was one of the places in the world about which I had harboured most illusions. The references to it in Mistral, the descriptions of it by innumerable English travellers, the knowledge that it has been a place of profane pilgrimage for lovers of poetry for centuries, all influence one to expect the sublime. I remembered, too, a story my mother used to tell me of her grandmother, who had travelled in France and Italy with her parents in the peace that followed Waterloo. The story concerned those albums fashionable a couple of generations ago, and in which you were asked to write down replies to a whole series of questions about your tastes: 'What is your favourite flower?' for instance, 'Who is your favourite poet?' 'What is your favourite colour?' and so on. To the question 'What is your favourite beverage?' my great-grandmother would always put the same consistent answer – 'Water from Petrarch's fountain at Vaucluse.' This story had lodged early in my mind, and with it a vision of clear, cold spring water bubbling in a crystal glass. I found in fact that the water at Vaucluse is of a crystalline clarity. It is the only feature of 'Petrarch's fountain' that cannot be spoilt.

The road from Avignon to the Fountain of Vaucluse takes one first past Le Thor, a small, self-satisfied-looking town still entered through its old rampart gate (now capped by an iron belfry) and possessing a twelfth-century church of severe grandeur, remarkable both for the magnificence of its portico and for the fact that the building has been in no way enlarged, modified or even ornamented since its completion in the year 1202. A little farther on you come to the shady, water-borne township of L'Isle-sur-la-Sorgue, a place built upon the ten banks of the river Sorgue, which, here dividing itself into five streams, gives this pretty town a false, fresh air of Holland. And then one reaches Vaucluse itself, or rather the assemblage of hotels, advertisement boards, cafés, open-air restaurants, booths selling souvenirs and *buvettes* selling lemonades, in which the original village of Vaucluse is quite engulfed. Vaucluse is situated at the base of a high cliff of rock, crowned by the bleak, rock-coloured ruins of the summer palace of the bishops of Cavaillon. It is from this rock ridge that the river Sorgue springs, emerging as a brackish gurgling pool from a low, grim cavern at the foot of the rock-face, a cavern such as one could fancy haunted by some beast of nightmare. To reach this spring you must walk for ten minutes or so from the village of Vaucluse, past the Hôtel Petrarque et Laure and the museum in a house said to have been inhabited by the poet, and on up the steep bank of the river. The banks of the Sorgue are moss-grown, and shaded by leaning trees; the river here is shallow and translucent, the water a visible blue. The long water-weeds that trail beneath the surface like strands of silken hair are emerald-green. The polished pebbles in the river-bed are small and white. But the beauty of this pre-Raphaelite scene is wrecked by the café chairs along the river-banks, the shacks and shanties, the eager touts. All has been commercialized and made vulgar. I feel in general no speck of sympathy for those professional admirers of the past who constantly lament the age we live in; but I confess to feeling beside Petrarch's fountain, as I have felt in Venice, that here was one place to which I had come a hundred and fifty years too late.

CHAPTER EIGHT

I

IF, IN AVIGNON, YOU CANNOT FAIL to be conscious of Viollet-le-Duc's architectural emendations (as well as of certain other nineteenth-century additions to the town), in Aix-en-Provence you may fancy yourself in a city unaltered since the French Revolution. Only the graceless cluster of allegorical figures on the huge fountain put up in 1860 in the centre of the *rond-point* at the western end of the Cours Mirabeau, only the ugly Municipal Casino erected near it in 1922, mar this illusion. For the rest the shadowy streets of this ancient capital of Provence seem as resolutely eighteenth century as those of the lovely Louis Quinze town of Semur-en-Auxois, and can be as imperturbable and quiet as the crescents and terraces of Bath. The peace of Aix is deceptive, however, for this is a university town; and in term-time the streets are as full of spinning bicycles as those of Oxford or Cambridge, the cafés seethe with chattering students, and the atmosphere is charged with all the intrigue, spite and petty gossip which is an integral factor of the life of any seat of learning. It is also, since the war, the scene of a musical festival which occurs in the high summer, though Aix is not, I think, a summer place. Smollett, visiting it on his way to Italy in 1765, disliked its situation 'in a bottom', encircled by hills 'which, however, do not screen it from the Bize'. 'If the air of Aix', he wrote, 'is disagreeably cold in winter, it is rendered quite insufferable in the summer, from the excessive heat, occasioned by the reflection from the rocks and mountains, which at the same time obstruct the circulation of the air'. Lady Blessington, stopping there more than fifty years later on a similar southward journey, was told that the climate was 'infinitely superior to that of Avignon', and was struck by the brilliance of the sun and the mildness of the February air. Aix as a matter of fact, is a place for the early spring, or for the sad, rich onset of a Provençal autumn.

I first visited Aix in such autumn weather, and the city was calm and empty, windless and agreeably warm. I began by staying at one of the old hotels in the Cours Mirabeau; but, after a day or two, living in this splendid shaded street, a sub-aqueous light filtering through the tall elm trees that meet overhead and are cut once a year in October, seemed very much like living at the bottom of a tank, an impression fostered by the many gurgling fountains of the city, three of them down the length of the Cours Mirabeau itself. I presently discovered and moved to one of the most excellent hotels in all Provence – the small, modern Hôtel Riviera, two kilometres from the centre of the city, up a turning off the Marseilles road. In the garden of this hotel you can eat out of doors under the plane trees, and sit and read in the seclusion of the garden but within sight of Mont Sainte-Victoire, to be seen at any moment of the day by raising your head from your book. From the Hôtel Riviera it is no distance to the walk to the Pont de l'Arc, and thence along that river's bank to the medieval Pont des Trois Sautets. Here I would wander late each afternoon, passing through a gentle rushy land-scape more like a Corot than a Cézanne; one or two people would be bathing in a pool of the river, while a black and beige spaniel would be slopping about at the water's edge. Beyond the Pont des Trois Sautets – a single arch of stone not unlike the old packhorse bridges of the Ridings of Yorkshire – there stands beside the dusty road a tall, narrow oratory of the Virgin Mary, put there in 1720. The oratories of Provence are as characteristic a part of the countryside as the calvaries of Brittany, or those big plain crosses of polished wood one finds at crossroads in the mountains of Savoy. They date from many periods, and when you come suddenly upon one it seems to mitigate or at least modify the innately pagan atmosphere of Provence.

These pleasant, dilatory rambles round the perimeter of Aix made one gradually familiar with the area, and with the setting of the city. The next time I came to Aix I lived in the countryside itself, near Le Tholonet. It was eight months later, and as I walked this time beside the Arc, the river was in heavy flood. This was an exceptionally rainy May, and all along the road from Palette, and on the track called La Petite Route du Tholonet, the crimson earth was curved and rumpled by the rain, like desert sands by wind. Mangy farm dogs limped angrily to shelter under the oak trees by the river-bank. The grass in meadows and hedges had grown rank with so much wet, and under a torn sky the tiny houses and cabins of Le Tholonet seemed crouching in high forests of greenery, so that as you worked your way towards them you felt like an insect among grass roots. On the afternoon that I arrived to spend some weeks at Le Tholonet the summit of Mont Sainte-Victoire was invisible from cloud, and the Arc was up over its own banks, the swirling water tugging viciously at low tree branches, the frantic twisted oak trees half submerged in the flood. On the Palette road the tamarisks, their fashionable-looking sprays of salmon flowers sparkling with rain, showed vaguely in the warm white mist, while the big strong flowering chestnut trees nearby looked positively waterlogged. These strange conditions, which gave to life round Aix the uncongenial atmosphere of an emergency, persisted several days. Then, at last, the sun shone explosively. Summer had begun.

It was during and after this rainswept interlude that I began exploring the country round Aix – the country in which Marius fought, Vauvenargues lived, Cézanne painted, and Émile Zola wrote. These explorations I varied by visits to the city itself, then gay with student life, and lit at evening by sunset skies which were as delicate as the colour of tea-roses, and which one glimpsed through the tall eighteenth-century windows of some acquaintance's apartment at dinner-time.

II

The village and château of Le Tholonet lie some six kilometres outside Aix-en-Provence, in a south-easterly direction. The village is small and lingering. Apart from the château, a large but unexciting building of the early eighteenth century with a white façade, painted shutters, and some legendary memories of the Marquis de Vauvenargues, the features of the village are a little church, described by Émile Zola in his novel of the Tholonet country, *La Faute de l'Abbé Mouret*, and the Restaurant Thomé, a rustic café to the outer wall of which is fixed a plaque recording an early automobile visit by King Edward VII, *'conduit par Monsieur Gras'*. The great beauty of Le

Tholonet, however, is not the château but the avenue of chestnut trees that leads up to it, between small canals fed by the river Arc. From the *cabanon* on the Petite Route where I was staying, you could see this avenue at all times of the day. From that distance it looked elegant, and very green; when you got close to it, and entered the mysterious world of cool shade cast by the branches of its giant trees, the avenue proved massive, even hefty. The boles of the trees are aged and irregular. Most of them are now permanently disfigured by large, deeply cut, superfluous inscriptions giving the names and States of origin of American soldiers stationed there at the time of the liberation of Provence.

One day I set out to walk to the next village to Le Tholonet, Beaurecueil. The way lies down the avenue, past the château, and then upwards beyond the church of Le Tholonet and the Cézanne memorial, a small bronze portrait relief affixed to a style. There had been a storm. The sky was pale, and stained with trailing cloud. To my left was a rocky skyline, peppered with stone-pines, and in some unexpected way a little reminiscent of the steep shores of Loch Ness. Along the roadside, and in the fields below the level of the road, were flowers: a profusion of wild gladioli in a stream-bed, dark blue and bright yellow flowers, and everywhere grey bushes of wild lavender. The earth was the colour of rust, and the big Invalides building at Beaurecueil looked cream-coloured against it. On the road, shiny with recent rain, there was no one in sight but a black-cotton peasant figure of indeterminate sex, and an empty bus which had quietly broken down at the turn of the road. I sat on a large rock beside the road, to study carefully the constant brooding companion of this and all other walks one could take in that direction – Mont Sainte-Victoire. From Aix and Tholonet this celebrated mountain had looked compact and high; as one walked towards Beaurecueil it appeared to unfurl, or to unfold like a screen, revealing itself as a long range rather than a mountain, and seeming somehow biscuit-thin. A landscape as famous, almost as notorious, as that of which Mont Sainte-Victoire is the centre requires great concentration to absorb: Mr Berenson has taught us that our attitude before a work of art should be that of a 'consumer', and certainly this process can fruitfully be applied to the works of nature too. Van Gogh's view of Arles, and Corot's view of Villeneuve-lès-Avignon, are of infinite value to us as enriching our own vision of those places; but none the less one wishes, with an obstinacy that may be independence or may also be conceit, to achieve a personal relation to such landscapes oneself. Sitting on a stone at Beaurecueil I tried to break free from Cézanne and his imitators, and to see Mont Sainte-Victoire for myself. I returned from this solitary walk somewhat encouraged, and with the determination to continue my attack.

When I got back to Le Tholonet I found a vast American car, one of those now so fashionable in France in which you cannot distinguish the front from the back as they nose their predatory way like satiated sharks through winding village streets and lanes. This car was stationary in front of the château: it bore a Moroccan registration plate, and seemed in some inexplicable way to block the whole great house from view. A fat and heaving lady and a big ugly child were posing for their photographs before the château, which looked, with its closed green shutters, disdainful and detached.

III

A few days later, as a further stage in my pursuit of Mont Sainte-Victoire, I set out from the house on the Petite Route du Tholonet to investigate the forest reservoirs of the ravine of the Infernect, some three-quarters of an hour's climb away. These sinuous artificial lakes – one formed by the Barrage François Zola which was built by the novelist's engineer father in 1843, the other of later date and forming a sheet of water locally known as La Petite Mer – lie concealed in a spur of the lofty foothills of the Mont Sainte-Victoire range, and I had heard much talk of their secluded aspect and strange beauty. The day was excessively hot. I and a friend set off at one o'clock, immediately after an early lunch, and without a siesta. In any climate a siesta is an aid; in Provence in such weather it is a necessity, and to abstain from it puts one into a nervously exhausted but slightly light-headed frame of mind.

To gain the ravine of the Infernect you do not pass through Le Tholonet, but take a track branching left over a high bank from the upper or main road to that village. In grilling sunshine we identified this pathway from a verbal description, and began to scramble up it into the hills. A little before the point at which the pathway leaves the road is another oratory, in which a small Virgin and Child, provincial, pretty, baroque figures, stand in a niche protected by a wire cage, and sheltered from the sun by the stiffly jutting boughs of a giant stone-pine, which casts over them a series of rigid, slatted shadows, as precise and delicate as the spandrels of a fan. At the foot of the statue a little bunch of flowers, squeezed through the wire, lay wilting in the noonday heat.

This heat, the stillness and silence of the early afternoon, a vague sense of exhaustion, and a vivid curiosity about our destination – for I had heard much of the allegedly eerie atmosphere of these bleak ravines in which Marius' barbarian prisoners are said to have quarried the stones for the construction of Aix – combined to infuse my mind with a mood of mystery, rather like the mood evoked in childhood by the reading of some fairy-tale. The first thing we came upon as we followed the pathway up the hillside was indeed rather hard to explain, since in this country every building that is not utterly ruined is put to some good use. It was a long, low habitable but entirely deserted house, with shuttered door and windows and rusted bars and bolts. Gnarled and aged olive trees encircled it, and under an old fig tree by the door were set a decaying table and a chair. The grass before the house was silky and bright green. Across it was a thicket of dark bushes, which half-concealed a natural rock formation like an arch. Beside the house were empty stables and an empty barn. Some considerable distance from this silent house stood another, from the back of which shrieks were issuing as rapidly as smoke from a chimney on fire. A gaunt old hag in a pudding-basin hat of yellow straw was tugging at two goats, one as black as black satin, one snow-white, which were trying to eat the vegetables in her straggling bean row. A couple of dogs were barking. The noise here was infernal.

Leaving this frenetic scene, we followed the path on and up, coming out into an open landscape the colour of wood-ash, charred as it seemed by the sun. On either side of the path whitish rocks and round boulders grew out of the ground, with slender silver firs upright between them; the earth on which we walked was springy with pale grey pine-needles and the dry twisted roots of old lavender bushes that had gripped and crept across the ground. The stones of the cart track were white, but streaked with stains of crimson soil brought down by the recent torrential rains. It was, I knew, in this extraordinary moon-struck country, where the traces of pathways dry away in summertime, and many of the boulders hide the mouths of subterranean caves, that the local Maquis had thriven in the last war. Aix was still full of tales of their heroism, violence and craft, of message systems through the mountains to Free French head-quarters at Marseilles, of cavern conferences, of the burning of forests by German troops in efforts to smoke out the conspirators, and of brutal executions. Several people at Le Tholonet had told me of how, bicycling into Aix to shop, they would suddenly see beside the road the corpse of a young man lying in long grass dabbled with blood; and I had myself noticed at least one tablet recording such German executions near a culvert on the Tholonet road. It seemed, indeed, an ideal country for the rather brigand-like activities of the Maquis. The fir trees and the boulders stretched away on every hand, still in the heat; the only sound was the occasional cry of a bird, the only movement, apart from our own lagging footsteps, the flopping of a butterfly alighting on a hot white stone. We went on and on, up and up, until a background noise of which I had been perhaps aware without paying any heed to it, crashed itself into my consciousness: I realized that it was the distant roar, then soon the nearby thunder, of the waters of the great dam.

The path turned a corner, and began abruptly to descend. To the right I saw a glint of water, and ahead of us beside the path, one of the oddest cafés in the world, hitched on to a ledge in the rock face and entirely roofed over by a gigantic plane tree. This café is some two or three hundred yards from the dam, down which a black wall of water was sluicing, smooth and sinister in the sun. Walking on above the dam, we looked down from the edge of a sheer cliff of rock on to a deep, silent lake, from which the water seemed hardly to be seeping away. The lake was Nile-green. An occasional breeze passed across its gleaming surface, combing it into silver lines, and sighing through the pine trees that grow right down to the water's edge. In the midst of these pine trees one aspen shivered constantly, as though it were alive, or being shaken by some creature at its root; this seemed otherwise a completely petrified forest. Frogs croaked on the margin of the lake. Walking a little way along the cliff top I was amazed to find to my left a second lake, much larger than the first. It led away into the heart of the forest like some wide liquid road. At first sight this lake lacked the eerie quality of the first one; no high cliff overhung it, and all its shores so far as I could see were gentle banks of green, with little bays, leafy promontories and tiny islets on which clusters of oak trees grew. It was like a lake seen by Poussin or by Claude. Alternating with the promontories, tongues of the lake-water stretched in amongst the forest trees, making an idyllic-looking, indented shore-line. Down on the bank, a boy was bathing, his bicycle leaning against a tree: but when I looked again after a further examination of the view the boy had gone, disappearing as though he were part of a mirage. We were left alone in the forest with the lakes. It was then that, in spite of the hour and the blinding sunlight, this forest began to seem as desolate and haunted as do many great French forests – Compiègne, Chantilly or the strange old forest of Maulnes in the Loiret near Ancy-le-Franc – and for which I know of no equivalent in England, certainly not in the picnicky, thrushy gaiety of Epping or the New Forest. In the background, above the rocks and the trees and lake, soared the familiar outlines of Mont Sainte-Victoire.

We scrambled down to the lakeside, and started off to walk round it – evidently a simple, half-hour's task, for we could quite clearly see the end of the lake from where we stood. But by the time we had fought our way through much undergrowth, been up to our knees in water, fallen over rotting logs and been forced into long detours by some unforeseen inlet or unexpected bay, we came to what had seemed to be the end: it proved merely a turn of the lake, and another expanse of water and another stretch of silent forest lay before us again. This happened several times during the afternoon. By five o'clock we had frankly abandoned the attempt to walk round the lake, for we had only just reached its end, the point at which the feeble waters of the Infernect trickle in. Opting for a steep but dry climb uphill, we clambered straight up one shore of the lake, and through a patch of burnt forest, clutching at blackened stumps of trees and at calcined branches that snapped as we went by. It was then that, pausing to gaze at the high orange cliff that closes this end of the ravine, I saw, far up in its face, a menacing and horrible dark cave, like a torn mouth in the rock, with no possible way of getting to it. It might have been a haunt of condors or vultures, and whereas the earlier part of the afternoon had been in fairy-story mood, this was something straight out of a nightmare: it had all the detail and vitality of a bad dream, and it generated that dream-like conviction that anything might happen next. I felt as though I were asleep, and paralysed in the knowledge that some nauseous clutch of giant birds of prey or vampire bats hung brooding in that cave all through the sultry afternoon, ready to swoop down across the forest and the lake at sunset, uttering their hideous cries.

We hastened up and on. At length, on the summit of the ridge, we reached a cheerful clearing where some woodmen were sawing the trunks of fallen trees. But soon we had to plunge once more into the darkest part of the forest, following a narrow footpath through thickets of young trees which met above one's head. There were occasional breaks in this tunnel, glades with pallid grasses growing in them here and there, and under some of the trees interesting-looking purple-pink flowers like leathery dog-roses grew low on the ground as though they had just been strewn there that afternoon; there was also a kind of campanula, a sharp-blue star on a long delicate stalk, drooping languidly. But everywhere in this part of the forest one had the sense of being carefully and malignly watched: these, I reflected, were indeed the woods of Westermain:

> Only at a dread of dark
> Quaver, and they quit their form:
> Thousand eyeballs under hoods
>   Have you by the hair.
> Enter these enchanted woods,
>   You who dare.

Avoiding the shores of the lakes, we managed to return to the dam and the pathway to Le Tholonet by another route. It was nearing twilight as we passed the cottage of the old hag with the goats, and the house in which nobody lived. The old woman and her goats, like the boy on the bicycle, had disappeared. The empty house, at which I glanced quickly as we sped by, looked even more mysterious and bewitched than in the afternoon. I did not like the contorted shapes of those olive trees in the twilight. I did not like that abandoned table, nor that expectant chair.

These wanderings in the country below Mont Sainte-Victoire – country joyfully explored by Paul Cézanne and Émile Zola in their youth, when in the late eighteen-fifties they would make delirious expeditions to the green barrage lake or to the inn at Le Tholonet in the company of their skylarking cronies, the brothers Baille – were varied by walking frequently into Aix itself. Here one could re-examine at leisure places and buildings visited cursorily the year before, and which I have often looked at since. This deliberate return to sights just growing familiar is an aspect of travel as enjoyable as the first shock of discovery; and it is interesting to observe the un-alterable power that certain places have to induce in one, on any occasion, an identical mood. On these morning walks the silhouette of Aix-en-Provence as one approached it was alone exciting. Starting early, before the impending heat of the day was more than a threat or a promise in the bright air, I would make my way at a leisurely pace towards this diffuse, umbrageous town, spread like a carpet at the foot of the Alpilles. Over its roofs and tree-tops a haze of vapour would be hovering, pierced here and there by shafts of morning light. These shafts would catch the stout octagonal tower of the cathedral, and the delicate, rigid spire of the Gothic church of Saint John of Malta, which rose like masts above a city moored in mist. Few sights on earth can be as beautiful as that of a town in Provence soon after dawn – the sight of Hyères, steep, untidy, silent and mysterious, from the hill of Saint-Bernard, for instance, or the medieval towns of the Durance valley – Sisteron, Digne, Forcalquier, Manosque – opalescent on their hilltops in the sunrise, beside the broad pale river and its shingly banks. In Provence, even more than elsewhere, it is rewarding to rise at dawn.

There are many ways of approaching Aix-en-Provence. Originally a major junction and halting-place on the Roman way from Fréjus to the Rhône, the old city has retained its importance as a nexus of main roads leading in all directions across Provence; you constantly find yourself driving through it on the way to somewhere else, or, if you are travelling cheaply, waiting to change buses in the Avenue Victor Hugo or the Cours Sextius. Walking in from Le Tholonet you enter the city from the east, along a dusty road that leads past the cemetery and the parade-ground, and displays all the elements typical of the outskirts of any southern French town – small villas shielded by high garden walls, sprays of bougainvillaea, eucalyptus trees, tin letter-boxes hanging beside secretive garden gates of painted sheet-metal which are just too tall for one to peep over on tiptoe. Then come the actual streets of Aix itself – a vegetable shop, a café on a corner, a garage with a pump; and soon you are in the midst of the city, in the small Place Forbin at the head of the Cours Mirabeau. Here, staring down the tunnel of dark trees much as Queen Anne gazes down Ludgate Hill to Fleet Street and the Strand, stands David d'Angers's statue of King René. This gentle, deprecatory, long-haired figure surmounts a plinth above an old fountain, from which clear water tumbles through four stone lions' masks. Crowned and robed, a sceptre in his right hand, in his left a bunch of those muscat grapes which he first introduced into Provence, a pile of books upon the plinth at his feet, this stone king of the eighteen-forties epitomizes the romantic view of the Middle Ages made popular in mid-nineteenth-century Europe by Alexandre Dumas and the imitators of Sir Walter Scott.

One of the finest streets in any European town, the Cours Mirabeau has four ranks of lofty trees down its length. It is flanked by the superb façades of the great private town houses of the Provençal nobility of the epochs of Louis Quatorze and Louis Quinze. Before these grandly conceived house fronts you have the impression you often get in Paris of the intensely private life they must conceal; of great courtyards, and frescoed staircases, of suites of rooms decorated with *gypseries* and lit by vast candelabra and by glittering chandeliers. Some of these houses, the Hôtel d'Espagnet in particular, with its grave, burdened caryatides, gargantuan in their proportions, have a provincial exaggeration about them which you would never find in Paris; yet by and large this beautiful *cours* conveys, as Lady Blessington wrote many years ago, 'more the idea of a quarter in some large capital than the principal street in a provincial town'.

In Lady Blessington's day the great houses of the Cours Mirabeau were still inhabited by the descendants of the families for which they had been built. These persons, members of the provincial nobility and aristocracy, would leave their country houses in the late autumn, and trundle off in their heavy coaches to pass the winter in Aix. Today few of these great town houses in the Cours Mirabeau are still lived in by one family. Most have been dissected into apartments, or leased to banks or other commercial firms. All down the street, in the shadows of the plane trees, are large cafés, and iron and wooden benches. Here you can sit and watch.

One of the most reposing sights to watch in any southern town are the people who fetch water from the fountains, old women and children stooping as they hold out a jug or a glass carafe, and pattering carefully away with it held full between their hands. In Aix the fountains can seem innumerable. That from which King René gravely presides over the city is the first of three placed at intervals along the centre of the Cours Mirabeau. The second is a *fontaine chaude*, producing lukewarm water, and this, like certain other fountains in the towns of Provence, is so moss-grown and ossified as to look lumpish and deformed. Another of these diseased fountains – for in spite of the green moss and delicate spidery ferns upon them, they have the appearance of a live organism suffering from a growth – is to be seen at Salon, and this specimen is even more sinister and cancerous; yet another, less repulsive from its cheerful situation, is in the pretty rural hill-town of Barjols, above Saint-Maximin-la-Sainte-Baume. These amorphous fountains have their admirers ('*charmante fontaine moussue du xviiime siècle*' is how the one at Salon is described), but one cannot help preferring the lovely fountain of the Four Dolphins, in the Place of that name at Aix, or that with winged creatures and lions' faces in the Place des Tanneurs.

While not precisely the axis of the city, the Cours Mirabeau does form the frontier between the earlier 'old town' of Aix, with its churches, markets and administrative buildings, and the newer residential quarter laid out in the south of the city by Cardinal Michel Mazarin, a seventeenth-century Archbishop of Aix, and brother of the cardinal-statesman of that name. To the north of the Cours three narrow streets lead deviously into the spacious Place du Palais de Justice, and this, on market days especially, provides a comforting change from the atmosphere of ennui and dark melancholy in which the tree-shadowed hotels of the Cours Mirabeau seem steeped. Here, on such mornings, the wide sunlit Place du Palais is chequered with untidy stalls and booths, and with hardware and pottery laid out upon the cobbled ground. Small country carts, with smaller donkeys harnessed to them, stand about. Everywhere is the pervasive exuberance of an outdoor market in the south, that vigorous sense of exploitation and intrigue, of swift adjustments and bargainings, of people eagerly discussing objects that they never mean to buy; the sense, in fact, of life, mobile and active, in contrast to the stagnant, dying world of the houses in the Cours Mirabeau, an old grand world of taste and style from which the blood has ebbed away. In places, as in persons, taste is seldom allied to vitality.

In addition to the pleasure of wandering listlessly through an open market, of walking up and down the little streets formed by the covered stalls, of watching and listening, of buying silk ties and cotton socks and toys and shining vegetables, there is another aspect of these scenes that is enticing: their essentially temporary quality. However long I stay in some such country town as Aix, I am invariably bewildered by the speed with which the weekly market comes and goes. The nocturnal, mushroom-like growth of the stalls is in itself mysterious; to walk on to the Campo at Siena of a Saturday morning, for instance, and find that supreme arc of paving, at which one was gazing by starlight a few hours before, transformed overnight into a busy encampment, a canvas town within a town, with lanes and junctions, and jostling vendors crying their wares; or to wake up in some Flemish town in the early morning and look casually down from one's window on to a square the day before quite grey and silent, now magically changed and filled with turbulent and coloured life. The impermanence of all things, which adds such interest and zest to the experiment of living, seems symbolized by the sudden, short, vociferous life of a street market, here one day, vanished the next.

In Aix-en-Provence the real fruit and vegetable market is held on the smaller Place de l'Hôtel de Ville. A solid-looking, squarish clock-tower is all that remains from the original Renaissance town hall, replaced in the seventeenth century by the fine building which still houses the Bibliothèque Méjanes, as well as the usual warren of French municipal offices smelling of used blotting-paper and dried ink. Access to the courtyard of this Hôtel de Ville is given by a wide elliptical archway, framing a splendid iron gate, rayed like the rising sun. Behind this gateway is the courtyard, and from the central door of this ascends a double staircase, dominated by a commanding baroque statue of the Maréchal de Villars, once Governor of Provence. This gateway, staircase and courtyard give one again the illusion of being in a far grander city than Aix, the illusion Lady Blessington noticed in the Cours Mirabeau, and which made earlier visitors compare Aix to Paris. This air of grandeur and of the great world is also to be found isolated in certain other buildings in this part of the city – the Hôtel d'Albertas most notably, the Hôtel d'Eguilles, and in the former palace of the archbishops of Aix next door to the Cathedral of Saint-Sauveur.

The Cathedral of Saint-Sauveur, a large unsatisfactory building, is a Romanesque parish church engulfed in a fourteenth-century Gothic cathedral. Its octagonal tower, which forms one of the features of the Aix skyline, was completed in the last century. At about the same time the niches of the west façade, emptied of saints at the Revolution, were filled with sentimental figures in the style of Viollet-le-Duc. Partially destroyed in the Wars of Religion, partially rebuilt in the seventeenth century, much titivated in the nineteenth, the cathedral lacks both coherence and personality, and is interesting chiefly for its possessions and its details – the nutwood doors of the western entrance carved by a sculptor of Toulon in 1504, and showing the four major prophets and the twelve sibyls; the set of Flemish tapestries from designs by Matsys originally in Canterbury Cathedral; the triptych of the Buisson Ardent, painted by Nicholas Froment towards 1465 for King René, and attributed for centuries to the hand of the king himself. This famous picture, with its glowing colours and the grave devotional portraits of the king and queen kneeling in the traditional posture of donors, one on each wing, hangs upon a wall of the nave of the cathedral, and is kept locked. The process of the unlocking of this triptych, and the creaking open of the ponderous wings, bring one emotions of expectancy and excitement similar to those caused by the sudden revelation of the Ivory Virgin in the quiet seclusion of the sacristy safe at Villeneuve-lès-Avignon.

Apart from these attributes of the Cathedral of Saint-Sauveur, the most impressive parts of it are the baptistery, and the simple Romanesque cloisters, where the arcading of twin pillars casts shadows in the sun. The baptistery, which apparently dates from the fifth century, and was renovated in 1577, is singularly beautiful, and comprises a circle of lofty grey-green marble pillars with Corinthian capitals, supporting an octagonal dome. These pillars, thought to be the remnants of some second-century Roman temple, have a staid nobility about them, standing there in the half-light which filters downwards from the dome, and glimmers on the early font sunk in the floor. The cloisters, which formed part of the eleventh-century church of Saint-Sauveur, are, by contrast, light and gay, and by walking through them you can reach the garden and courtyard of the former palace of the archbishops of Aix. The atmosphere of this courtyard, and of the museum of tapestries now installed on the first floor of the palace, has a quality of complete loneliness and immemorial peace rarely found in any town, even in Provence.

V

I scarcely know what elements combine to produce the strong effect of fascination exerted by the old *archevêché* of Aix. A noble building facing on to a very large courtyard, in which palm trees flourish, it occupies the site of the medieval palace of the archbishops, pulled down and rebuilt by Cardinal Grimaldi in 1648. Entering this courtyard from the cathedral cloister, which is small and harbours a colony of pieces of early Christian carving, propped and stood against the walls, it seems immense, and yet, by some trick of proportion, intimate and still. The atmosphere of courtyard and palace is at once elating and infinitely sad. I have never been over this museum without finding it entirely empty of visitors; the whole place seems isolated in time, lonely and private. You cross the courtyard with a sense of intrusion.

The main door of the palace, ordinarily ajar, admits you to a dim, double-ramped, echoing staircase, curving up superbly to the first floor, its wrought-iron balustrade a chain of harps. Urns of monumental size ornament this staircase, giving it an air of cold and funerary grandeur; and at the top of it a door labelled *Musée* is unbolted by a severe-looking lady, in answer to a pressure on the bell. Through this doorway lie the six spacious rooms – doubtless the chief state apartments of the archbishops of Aix – with tall windows overlooking the courtyard below. These rooms, which turn the inner corner of the building so that the last are almost at right angles to the first, were redecorated under Louis XVI. They contain good *boiseries* and marble overmantels, and are furnished with excellent examples of Louis Quinze and Louis Seize commodes and chairs. On the walls is a quantity of somewhat nondescript French pictures of the seventeenth and eighteenth centuries, mainly of religious subjects, and the tapestries of Beauvais unearthed in the palace in 1849. These are the tapestries one has come to see.

The centrepiece of this compact collection is the set of illustrations to the life of Don Quixote, woven at Beauvais under the direction of Oudry and Besnier from cartoons designed by Charles Natoire in 1735. These cartoons still exist, at Compiègne, and of the ten tapestries done from them nine are here in Aix. Free, bold and animated, these Cervantic scenes are set against imaginative architectural backgrounds. Their borders are agreeably simple, and in marked contrast to a rival series of Don Quixote's adventures, that executed by the Gobelins from designs by van Coypel, and notable for the intense elaboration of their settings. Second in importance to the Don Quixote tapestries are the three 'Jeux russiens', in which gay-looking boys wearing fur hats dance with Boucheresque village girls against snowy landscapes. The complete series of these Russian games were six in number, and were designed for the Beauvais factory in 1769 by Le Prince on his return from years spent in the north of Europe. The other tapestries include six classical designs after Berain, and some exceedingly pretty 'Grotesques', woven on a deep yellow ground, and showing personages in romantic feathered head-dresses grouped beneath draped porticos, or between great vases of flowers. The pale clear colours of the tapestries, and the extreme vigour of their designs, seem to keep these rooms, which would otherwise be sombre, strangely alive. The same cannot, alas, be said of the works of art – several of them of first-rate quality – interned in the Musée Granet, the official painting and sculpture museum of the City of Aix.

The Musée Granet, named from the Aixois painter François-Marius Granet, who bequeathed more than five hundred paintings to the municipality when he died in 1849, and whose portrait by Ingres is perhaps the most beautiful single painting in the whole museum, is housed in the buildings of the old Priory of Saint John of Malta, beside the church dedicated to that saint in the seventeenth-century quarter of the town. Hitherto uncatalogued, the museum is at length undergoing a much-needed reorganization, and many of its forty-three rooms are now closed to the public. It was, in old days, a most depressing place, a jumble of pictures skied about its dingy rooms, its ground floor a confusing forest of Celto-Ligurian, Graeco-Roman and early Christian statuary. One of the best public collections in the French provinces, it is now in the hands of an able curator, who aims to make it coherent, intelligible, and worthy of the ancient capital of Provence.

VI

As well as the romantic Ingres portrait of François Granet, shown standing in a black cloak, his throat bare, against a Roman landscape and clear sky, the museum of Aix contains portraits of other *hommes illustres*, or as British travellers would use to call them, 'worthies', born in the city. The tiny Musée Arbaud contains more. But in neither of these collections, nor indeed anywhere in France, is there an authentic or indisputable likeness of the most interesting of all the sons of Aix, Luc de Clapiers, second Marquis de Vauvenargues.

Born at Aix-en-Provence in 1715, dying half-blind in Paris thirty-two years later, this gentle, short-lived and sad philosopher was never painted. The portrait labelled his in the Musée Arbaud, like the bust by Ramus once thought to be of Vauvenargues in the Bibliothèque Méjanes, is now considered to represent one or other of his two brothers, or even his father, hero of the great plague year of 1720-21, when more than seven thousand people died in Aix, and when, by his able administration, Joseph de Clapiers saved the city from chaos. The only traces of Vauvenargues at Aix are the remains of the old fifteenth-century town house of the Clapiers family near the Hôtel de Ville, a notebook in his writing in the Bibliothèque Méjanes, and a copy of the first edition of his *Introduction à la connaissance de l'esprit humain* in the same library with manuscript annotations by himself and by Voltaire. To find any more evocative association, you must go some nine miles outside Aix to a lonely valley below Mont Sainte-Victoire. Here, on a wooded hillock, sits the square Renaissance Château de Vauvenargues supported by battlements of a still earlier epoch, and surrounded by a billowing sea of trees. In this castle, which had come into the possession of his father's family through a sixteenth-century marriage settlement and brought with it little but wild uncultivated land and certain rights over the barren reaches of the nearby Mont Sainte-Victoire, Luc de Clapiers spent each spring and summer of his boyhood. Here he would sit reading Plutarch and Seneca in French translations, working himself up into such a passion of excitement at the old heroic deeds which they relate that he would rush out of his room to stride up and down the terrace in a state of fever. As a grown man, however, he had small use for life at the Château de Vauvenargues: 'I could not, in any case,' he once wrote, 'support the solitude and ennui of a country winter.' Nor did this least characteristic of all Provençaux care greatly for life in his native city, or even for Provence itself.

'It is true, my dear Mirabeau,' Vauvenargues wrote in January 1739, to the author of *L'Ami des hommes* (one of his only intimates in Aix), 'that I do not love Provence; but this is not due to reflection, I should hate its failings less if mine were ignored there . . . if people approved of me more, I should find fault with them less. I am conscious of a constant opposition between my own character and the ways of this country'. Thoughtful by nature, subjective and pessimistic through ill-health, resenting the constraint of family life and yet loathing the frivolity of his equals and contemporaries, Vauvenargues felt entirely out of place in the society of Aix, where artificiality of manners alternated with the full-blooded Provençal buffoonery of spectacles such as the procession of the Fête-Dieu which Marmontel saw and criticized. From his early readings, Luc de Clapiers had imbibed noble ideals of fame and glory. On these he unsuccessfully tried to base his life. His father, who disapproved of his bookish tendencies, put him into the fashionable and extravagant Régiment du Roi. He stayed an officer ten years; then, after trying to become a diplomat, and thwarted in every direction by his ill-health, his bad eyesight, his debts and lastly by an attack of smallpox, he veered slowly towards literature again, becoming, as it were, a writer from frustration. '*Tout homme qui n'est pas dans son véritable caractère n'est pas dans sa force*' is one of his most famous maxims, and it closely applied to his own life; for it was only when he began seriously to write down his conclusions on existence that his genius emerged. In 1746, the year before he died, Vauvenargues published in Paris an *Introduction à la connaissance de l'esprit humain, suivie de réflexions et de maximes*. It was little noticed outside the circle of Voltaire and of Vauvenargues' few close friends. Republished posthumously in 1747, the book went through four more editions, each slightly augmented, in the next hundred years. In 1857 appeared Gilbert's comprehensive edition of Vauvenargues' published and unpublished works, brought to the attention of the public by Sainte-Beuve. Since that time the study of Vauvenargues' *Maxims*, his *Characters*, and his *Dialogues*, and the analysis of his contribution to human thought have been growing steadily until, now recognized as one of the thinkers who unconsciously helped to achieve the great revolution in the human spirit for which Rousseau and the Encyclopedists are chiefly responsible, he has won the fame for which he yearned.

Because he died so young, because his sensibility and ill-health probably precluded his making any mark in company, and because for ten years he took part in the foreign campaigns of Louis XV, or hibernated in provincial garrison towns, Vauvenargues is a man of whom we have very few first-hand accounts. Apart from one or two sections of his *Characters* in which he seems to have been describing himself, he only appears in such passages of his contemporaries' writings as the *Memoirs* of Marmontel or Voltaire's funeral eulogy of French officers killed in the war of 1741 (which inexplicably includes amongst heroic deaths in battle that of a Chevalier de Boufflers aged ten). Marmontel, who first met Vauvenargues with Voltaire, considered him to be in spirit and character the most attractive man he had ever known; 'the good, the virtuous, the wise Vauvenargues', he calls him, a man 'cruelly treated by Nature in so far as his body was concerned, he was, as regards the soul, one of her rarest masterpieces', 'I used to think,' he adds, 'that in him I was seeing Fénelon, suffering and infirm.'

Marmontel said that Vauvenargues' conversation was even more subtle and eloquent than were his writings. Voltaire described him as concealing brilliance beneath the simplicity of a timid child. '*C'était un vrai philosophe*,' Voltaire wrote in 1764 to Le Clerc de Montmercie, an inferior poet who, loving Vauvenargues, had devoted fifty-six lines to his memory in the long adulatory poem *Voltaire*, which he published in that year; '*il a vécu en sage, et est mort en héros, sans que personne en ait rien su.*' The other surviving tributes of his friends, all pitched in such terms of generalized praise, do not help us to know how Vauvenargues looked, or spoke, or, indeed, really lived. From his own works we can glean no more than his strikingly humane and intelligent attitude to life. Like Rousseau, Vauvenargues was convinced of the supreme importance of the emotions, putting sentiment and passion above reason and common sense. He combined a perfect faith in the potentialities of human heroism with a thorough understanding of human weakness. He loathed cynicism, ridicule, and scorn. He hated the sneering psychology of La Rochefoucauld. At once the enemy of epicureanism and of stoicism, he condemned both those who live for pleasure only, and those who regard life as already overshadowed by the tomb. 'To execute great things,' runs one of his wisest and most-quoted maxims, 'one must live as though one were never going to die.' 'The thought of death deceives us,' he writes elsewhere, 'for it makes us forget to live,' and 'One cannot judge life by a falser standard than that of death.' But though his maxims, his letters and his scraps of notes teach us to understand his mind, the actual personality of Vauvenargues remains spectral and enigmatic. Part of an age which produced the magnificent self-revelations of Jean-Jacques Rousseau, the tremendous documentation of Voltaire, Luc de Clapiers seems as elusive, as intangible as a wraith. Since familiarizing oneself with the place in which a man has lived can sometimes give one a sense of increased intimacy with him, I had long been anxious to make a pilgrimage to the village and château of Vauvenargues. When I had done so I found I felt no closer to him than before.

Most illogically, I had never been to Vauvenargues when I was staying near by at Aix-en-Provence, and it was only when settled at the other end of the country, at Hyères one April, that I found an occasion to go. Having to take the evening aeroplane at Marignane, which involved driving through Aix on the way, I thought this an admirable opportunity to satisfy my curiosity about Vauvenargues. I was accompanied by three friends who were coming to see me off at the airport, and we arranged to take a picnic lunch to Vauvenargues. As I have said elsewhere in this book, I am firmly convinced that sightseeing should be done alone; particularly sightseeing as evocative and ambiguous in purpose as this projected visit to Vauvenargues. As it was, the extreme gaiety, and to a lesser degree the emotional tensions, of this particular picnic detracted sharply from the object of the expedition. We had an enchanting day in a Provençal valley, and one ended it knowing nothing more about Vauvenargues.

April at Hyères, with the gardens lush with flowers, pale red camellia petals littering the ground, has a wonderful quality of intensity about it which even the height of summer cannot rival. When we left that morning the sun was brilliant, and the shadows shortening all along our road. On the way we stopped in a village to drink a bottle of wine beneath an arbour heavy with wistaria bloom; skirting Aix, we reached Vauvenargues, as we had intended, in time for luncheon. The valley in which the hamlet and castle of Vauvenargues are wedged lies between the steep Le Lubaou on one side, Mont Sainte-Victoire on the other. At the bottom of this valley a stream wanders along through a wild, rock-strewn wood. Above and out of this wood there rises the small compact castle of Vauvenargues, a square Renaissance building on a hillock like a nursery fort, made yet higher by medieval defence-works, and half-hidden in a cascade of branching trees. The castle faces down the valley; on one side of it is a small chapel. Below the main gate a sloping grass bank runs to the edge of the wood. It was here, at the foot of the path leading up to the gate, that we unstrapped the big plated picnic hamper. A picnic is one of the most difficult meals in the world to manage well; to make it not merely enjoyable but even decent demands considerable intelligence and taste.

After we had washed the plates and glasses in a bucket of water brought from the stream by an old man, drunk coffee and brandy, and dozed, it seemed time to tackle the question of getting into the château, which looked empty and was evidently locked. At this moment a handsome girl with bright dark eyes, and shining dark hair to her shoulders, dressed in blouse and breeches, appeared from the wood. She was following two spaniels, and when we asked her whether we could look inside the house she equivocally replied that there was nothing to see. Her husband and herself, owners, we presently discovered, of two Marseilles nightclubs, were having the château stripped and restored before taking up residence there. As we persisted in questioning her, she led us up the paths through the gate and across the little formal garden below the terrace on which Vauvenargues used to walk. This balustraded terrace is approached by a flight of some twenty wide stone steps, leading to a solid, monumental doorway, on each side of which are three large windows protected by iron bars. Inside the door is a vast, chilly stone hall, with a white stone staircase going to the upper floor. The rooms, as she had warned us, were quite empty of furniture, but they contained the plaster work called *gypseries*, good overmantels, and wall-coverings of stamped 'Spanish' leather. But the interior of the château lacked personal character, and did not fulfil the mysterious promise of the exterior, defended by its gates and trees. From without it seemed as romantic as the villa at Belcaro seen from the ramparts of Siena; inside it was disappointing and lacked atmosphere. As we were leaving, the young lady (who had confided to us that it was probable that the title went with the castle of Vauvenargues, and could be used by its new owners) ran upstairs and returned with four copies from what she told us was a store of nineteenth-century editions of Vauvenargues' works which she had discovered in an upper attic. Thanking her for her generosity, we left her and arrived later in the evening at Marseilles.

Seated in the aeroplane as it rose into the night and circled over the shimmering Étang de Berre, the lights of Martigues on the ground below us looking like fireworks, I began to wonder why I had so utterly forgotten Vauvenargues the moralist during that happy afternoon. Cutting the book in my lap with a visiting card I began to re-read his maxims at random. I could hardly believe what I saw: '*Le plus beau jour de la vie d'une femme est celui de ses noces ou de sa viduité*'...'*Il est des hommes qui sont leur plus cruel ennemi.*'... The insipidity of the maxims seemed equalled only by their smug air of worldly knowledge. I looked quickly at the title-page and I saw that we had been given not the *Maxims* of Luc de Clapiers, but the *Méditations philosophiques et aphorismes* of a Comte d'Isoard-Vauvenargues who had published his paltry conclusions upon life in the year 1856. By some sad piece of irony the new *châtelains* of Vauvenargues, friendly and enthusiastic though they were, could not distinguish between the one writer and the other. I perceived that it was altogether too late to pursue the spirit of the great Vauvenargues in that lonely valley between the mountains of Le Lubaou and of Mont Sainte-Victoire.

I realize now that one error was to have seen over Vauvenargues in the afternoon, for that is never a good time to look at anything. Indeed, it is hard to know just what the early part of the afternoon is good for; since childhood I have wished that there was some way of abolishing the hours between two and five. In Provence one should aim to arrive in an unknown town towards nightfall. But is not this true of all travelling – whether you are bound for some quiet half-timbered manor house in Shropshire with a trout stream flowing round it, or to a villa on the heights of Bellosguardo; to a farm in Virginia, or a stony island in the Skagerrak; to a cocoa plantation in the West Indies or to a dead port upon the Zuyder Zee? In every case evening enhances the excitement of arriving, for evening brings out the natural mystery that lurks in all long-inhabited places, to try to decipher, or at least to recognize, which seems a chief purpose, as it is a chief enjoyment, of living. It was at evening that I first saw one of the most engaging and, I believe, least visited of the minor towns within reach of Aix-en-Provence – the town of Apt, some fifty kilometres away across the Durance, in the neighbouring department of Vaucluse.

Built along the southern bank of the river Coulon, a tributary of the wide Durance, Apt (which houses, the *Blue Guide* tells us, some six thousand citizens) is set amongst hills with fruit trees, oaks and chestnuts growing on them. Behind it rears the Lubéron, one of the highest mountains of this region of Provence. Once a Roman station of some minor consequence, and said to be the place in which the Emperor Hadrian's favourite horse, Borysthenes, expired, Apt has a cathedral built in the eleventh and thirteenth centuries, dedicated to Saint Anne whose relics it is thought to house.

Like the alleged body of Mary Magdalen at Saint-Maximin, and like those of her companions at Les-Saintes-Maries-de-la-Mer, these relics were for centuries objects of pilgrimage for pious persons from other parts of France. Anne of Austria, for instance, came down to Apt in 1660, to fulfil a vow made to her patron saint. This royal visit occurred during the episcopate of the bishop Modeste de Villeneuve des Arcs, and the Queen promised eight thousand livres for the completion of the chapel of Saint Anne, begun five years earlier;

designed by La Valfenière, this chapel, the first on the left as you enter by the cathedral's western door, has a fine cupola and contains some Italian marble reliefs. Anne of Austria also contributed a large gold statue of Saint Anne, and an eagle almost as large studded with emeralds, but these objects, like much of the cathedral plate, did not survive the French Revolution, and are not to be found amongst the cathedral treasure today kept in the sacristy. Until the Revolution, Apt was the seat of a bishopric. Its medieval history was that usual to such Provençal towns, of recurrent wars and skirmishes for lands and title between the prince-bishops of Apt and the local seigneurs. Today a place of greatly diminished interest, Apt retains one lovely building which can serve as a reminder of the town's former importance. This is the episcopal palace, begun about 1752 and finished nine years before the outbreak of the Revolution. It was to see this palace and this cathedral that I set off from Aix one damp October evening shortly after six o'clock.

Halts included, the slow bus journey from Aix to Apt takes two and a half hours. The road lies through the shallow open country bordering the Durance, past Cadenet on its ridge, past the sad Renaissance castle of Lourmarin, through the little burg of Bonnieux and thence to Apt. As we crossed the bridge over the Durance the sun was setting. Between the dove-grey rocks and the smooth round stones of the river's bed the pools and tongues of water glittered like flame in the reflected light. Even the tarmac, curving away towards Cadenet, and slippery from recent rain, shone like a road on fire. Lourmarin, in its formal garden, looked dismal and sinister in the failing light. The mountain of the Lubéron seemed menacing the road. Then we were passing the hillsides near Apt, and finally the bus came to a stop in the middle of a wide square. On the left was a low wall below which ran the Coulon, and on the right a row of plane trees and buildings amongst which the façades of the town's two hotels, glassed-in verandas before them, were unmistakable. Having deposited myself and my luggage, the bus rattled on down the main street of the town. Lights were burning in the hotel windows. Under the plane trees, in the twilight, men and boys were playing bowls.

I chose, mistakenly, the larger of the two hotels, under the impression that it would be more comfortable. According to the guide-book, with its unfailing mass of statistical information, the Hôtel du Louvre has thirty-five rooms. I felt that I must have passed the doors of all of them by the time I had followed the hotel-keeper along a series of those dingy, confusing, suddenly twisting narrow corridors peculiar to French provincial hotels. The room which I was finally allotted, and which I later found to my cost to have damp, or at any rate unaired, sheets, proved to be straight over the front door by which I had come in; one would have supposed it easier to reach than by the maze through which I had been guided. The corridors and stairs and rooms of the hotel had the red hexagonal tiling common to most small Provençal hotels and houses. These had lately been beeswaxed and smelt clean and fresh. I seemed to be the only person who had been in the hotel for years, but at dinner, served outside under the glass veranda, I found a tawdry, slatternly-looking couple who had with them, by way of contrast, a spruce and spoilt white dog. At dinner we were given (there seemed no question of a menu) that particularly nauseating intestinal dish called *andouillettes*. After this meal I set out to look round the town. Although the river-bed was almost dry, the air along the stone quays seemed dank and chilly. I wondered whether, in the event, I was going to like Apt.

But Apt at night soon proved informal and exciting. The town was, to begin with, comfortingly ill-lit. Here and there a street or wall lamp showed a feeble lustre, making a wavering patch of light which left the objects beyond its limits ambiguous bluish silhouettes. I passed a large dog sitting steadfastly on its haunches, and a stationary pony with a cart. The houses of Apt were closed, their doors bolted and their windows shuttered against insects and the sharp air of the autumn night. In some of the few shop-windows, near the cathedral, blinds were pulled down; in others the merchandise displayed, made colourless by night, could just be seen. In many of the narrow streets were bars and cafés, and from the open doors of these the light fell upon the pavement in yellow blocks, or was filtered through the quivering bead curtains. Noise as well as light emerged from these cafés, making a contrast to the silent streets of Aix which I had quitted. There were murmurs, and bursts of adolescent laughter in the darkness, the glow of cigarette-ends and the light sound of the bowls.

Turning away from the Quai de la Liberté, and the dry river-bed of the Coulon which seemed like a pale, anonymous no-man's-land below it, I wandered towards the cathedral, passed beneath a colonnade near by, and began to return to the Place de la Bouquière, on to which faced my hotel. I found myself instead in another open *place*, smaller and more silent, isolated in the lamplight and the autumn night. Here, beneath and against a plane tree, three handcarts, in mysterious confabulation, stood tipped up. The only other features of the square were some more plane trees and a pair of late eighteenth-century fountains of surprising elegance and beauty. Each of these was in the form of a laughing naked child standing astride a large dolphin which balanced on a plinth. The children were holding the dolphins' tails, and from the mouths of the fish two streams of water tumbled into two basins below. At the back of these fountains, which stood symmetrically level with one another across the end of the *place*, was a stone terrace with a geometrically patterned iron balustrade, and approached by two flights of stone steps. Behind the balustrade of the terrace I could see dimly the tall and well-proportioned windows and the great door of an eighteenth-century hôtel which stood there, grand and inanimate-looking, beneath the night sky. Everything about this square – the carts, the trees, the lamps, the shuttered windows of the palace – seemed frozen and lifeless. The tinkling water of the dolphins was the only sound I heard. In this building I recognized the palace ostentatiously begun in 1752 by Monseigneur Félicien-Bocon de la Merlière, and completed in 1780 by his scholarly successor, Monseigneur de Cély, the last bishop of Apt. I had learned something of both these ecclesiastics and of their episcopates from the Abbé Boze.

VIII

If one believes the intricacies of human action and motive to be the most fascinating study in the world – if, in other words, one is a devotee of Balzac – one cannot fail to find a ceaseless interest in browsing through the detailed records of dead lives; the memoirs and the letters of quite private persons, books of local and family history, the publications of county record societies, and those vividly compiled volumes of state trials without which no English country-house library was once considered complete. I would personally include the history of bishoprics in this category, for, peeping between the lines of deliberate eulogy by some bland diocesan historian, one can catch glimpses of that world of intrigue and ambition, saintliness and pettiness which Balzac and Trollope have each, in his own country, examined and revealed. We can observe the contrast between one prelate and his predecessor, and deduce the intrigues of some ambitious vicar-general to succeed his bishop. We come, too, upon arresting scenes as when during the plague of 1721 the venerable Monseigneur de Foresta left his palace in Apt, and mounting barefoot to the hill of Tauleri, solemnly blessed the town and diocese whilst the citizens of Apt prostrated themselves upon their roof-tops.

It was for these reasons that I had been particularly glad to find, in a bookshop in the Quartier des Fusteries at Avignon, a copy, bound in black and lemon-yellow marbled boards, of the history of the Church of Apt by the Abbé Boze. This book, which Mérimée mentions in his *Notes d'un voyage* of 1835, was written, printed and produced at Apt five years after the final Restoration of Louis XVIII. It was compiled with a variety of motives: to instruct the citizens of Apt in their local history, to idealize the old order in the persons of a calm, benign series of bishops of Apt, to expose the sacrilege committed in the cathedral during the Terror, and finally to edify the faithful by prolix accounts of the legendary lives of the saints of Apt: Saint Auspicius, the first bishop, Saint Elzéar de Cabran, and the virgin saint, Delphine. Even the author felt that this hagiological section of his book took up an excessive space, for he apologizes for it in his preface, explaining that he had thought it better to expand rather than to abridge these three biographies. But the latter portion of the volume, comprising concise histories of the episcopates of each bishop of Apt, is full of interest, especially when it describes the rebuilding of the bishop's palace, one of the last architectural expressions of the strength of the Church in France before 1789.

In December 1751, near the beginning, that is to say, of the long reign of Madame de Pompadour, there died in the old palace at Apt, Jean Baptiste de Vaccon, bishop of the diocese for the past twenty-eight years. The elevation of Monseigneur de Vaccon, the nephew and the grand-vicar of his predecessor Monseigneur de Foresta, who had resigned in his favour shortly after the abatement of the great plague of 1721, had been a clear case of nepotism, but the modesty and saintliness of the new bishop had seemed to justify his appointment. He was modest, popular and austere, living frugally in the old medieval bishop's palace and using his revenues for the poor of his diocese. People went so far as to credit Monseigneur de Vaccon with miraculous powers, for when, during the serious flooding of the town by the Coulon in 1748, he had approached the swiftly rising waters which seemed to be threatening the whole of Apt, and blessed them, they began to ebb. The good bishop's successor, who took over the diocese in August 1752, was a very different type of man.

Born at the Château de la Merlière in the Dauphiné, Monseigneur de la Merlière was, at forty-two, an imposing, active ecclesiastic, distinguished in face and bearing, elegant, ambitious and successful. A missionary and a theologian, he was noted for the able extempore sermons in which he would flay the Philosophes and condemn the moral depravity of the day. Clearly obsessed with a sense of his own importance, Monseigneur de la Merlière took immediate steps to build himself a suitable palace in his new diocese. This was partly constructed from materials of the old palace which, himself moving to the seminary, he ordered to be torn down; but when these stones proved insufficient, the new prelate decided on the demolition of a nearby church, desecrated some years earlier, but of which the people of Apt were fond. The destruction of this church was resented in the town. Together with other somewhat equivocal acts of the bishop, it did not increase his popularity with his flock and we may fancy that when Monseigneur de la Merlière's health began to fail, as early as 1758, few of his parishioners were really sorry. Running his diocese by decrees and letters, soon unable to even appear in public to preach, the bishop managed to hold out for another twenty years. At length in 1778 he resigned, leaving to his successor a quantity of thorny problems, amongst them that of what to do with the unfinished structure of the bishop's palace which, ornamented on the garden side with a pompous tablet declaring that the illustrious doctor Félicien-Bocon de la Merlière, Bishop and Prince of Apt, had placed it there in July 1754, to record the rebuilding of the palace for himself and his successors, had otherwise 'almost everything imperfect, owing to lack of time or money'. The next, who was also the last, prince-bishop of Apt did not hesitate to complete the work. Within two years the new palace at Apt was finished and ready. As it turned out, it was ready in time for the French Revolution.

Monseigneur de la Merlière had been known as the enemy of the Philosophes. His successor, Laurent-Michel-Eon-de-Cély, a native of Bayeux, was a man so scholarly and retiring, so much more fond of arranging his collections of antique coins and medals than of preaching in his diocese, that the ignorant Aptesians suspected him of strong sympathies with freethinkers and agnostics, of being in fact himself a follower of the Philosophes. One of Monseigneur de Cély's first steps was to suppress the seminary of Apt, to increase the number of priests in his diocese by aiding them with the economies thus made, and to use the rest of this money, the large sum of sixty thousand francs, in completing his palace. This he appears to have done with dictatorial efficiency. Houses which faced on to the square before the palace were demolished. The palace gardens were altered and enlarged. The terrace with its wrought-iron balustrade, its steps and its fountains, was constructed. In 1780 the bishop could move in. It was not for long.

As prudent – or should we say as timorous? – as he was retiring, the Bishop of Apt was one of the very first ecclesiastics to leave France before the end of 1789. The Abbé Boze, as loyal to this last bishop as to his predecessors, explains that Monseigneur de Cély's passion for natural history and for classical antiquities made him choose Italy as the country of his emigration. He settled happily amongst the scholarly ecclesiastics of the court of Rome, only moving to Naples when the revolutionary armies entered Italy. Here he made a famous expedition to the crater of Vesuvius, returning again to Rome where he attached himself to the household of Mesdames de France, the aunts of Louis XVI, and later leaving with them for southern Italy. At Naples, *les tantes du roi*, their suite, and the Bishop of Apt, boarded a boat which took a month to make its way northwards to Trieste, a passage so unpleasant that on landing first one and then the other of the royal sisters died. The Bishop of Apt found himself stranded in Trieste. He was asked to resign his bishopric, which, under the papal concordat with Napoleon, was soon afterwards abolished. Returning to France in 1803 he settled down, not in his fine new palace at

Apt, but in a small house and garden at Marseilles, where he died in penury in 1815.

Such is the history of the palace of the bishops of Apt, which took so long to build, and was finished too late. Today it houses the offices of the mayor and the sub-prefect of the district. Bicycles are propped on the terrace, typewriters chatter within its rooms. But at night it looks civilized and sophisticated, silent in the lamplight while the dolphin fountains flow.

CHAPTER NINE

I

THE GOLD-ENCRUSTED RELICS OF Saint Anne in the basilica at
Apt, those of Saint Martha in her church below the Rhône bridge at
Tarascon, and the bones unearthed by King René at Les-Saintes-
Maries-de-la-Mer, made of each of these places an important centre
of pilgrimage in Provence. But by far the most popular and, as it was
thought, the most undoubtedly rewarding objects for pilgrims in this
part of the world were the body of Saint Mary Magdalen preserved in
a crypt of the great Dominican abbey at Saint-Maximin-du-Var, and
the cave in which she traditionally lived and died, up on the
neighbouring mountain of the Sainte-Baume.

Situated on the direct route that goes from Aix-en-Provence to
Brignoles and thence down to the Riviera coast, Saint-Maximin-du-
Var is vaguely familiar to the thousands of holiday tourists who
whirl through it in their motor-cars, or possibly stop there for half
an hour to eat a meal. I had always wanted to settle for a day or two
in this town, and to look at the abbey thoroughly, and so I arrived
there one summer's morning on what proved to be a day of intense
heat. The hotel had high windows, with tubs of oleanders outside
them on the pavement, and red shiny tiles like the hotel at Apt.
Saint-Maximin, however, is neither an intimate nor an enticing
town, and as the afternoon drew on I decided that it might be a good
thing to go out into the surrounding country for a walk. By leaving
some place one does not really like for a few hours, and then returning suddenly to it, one can sometimes modify one's feeling of
antipathy. The sense of strangeness is replaced by that of recognition. Choosing as a random aim a village on a distant hilltop, like
a hill in Italy, I began to walk out of the town. This village had
a quality of mirage about it, for it seemed firmly to recede as I
approached.

It was seven o'clock in the evening, and the fields were almost empty. The air smelt of hay as well as of vine leaves. On either side of the path the vines stretched out in level ranks across the plain. Their leaves, sprayed lately, were flecked with stains of turquoise blue. Outside a cabin in the middle of one of the vineyards, two or three people were stooping over the vines. By the door was a water-pump, worked by a yellow horse that was trudging round and round, and, further on, a labourer and his son had finished work. They were leaning on their pitch-forks of bright wood, looking into the sunset. In reply to a question of mine, the man pointed up at the shrine of the Sainte-Baume high on the flank of that famous mountain, which stood square on the horizon like a cliff. In the Var (as in the Vaucluse and the Bouches-du-Rhône) mountains look solitary and powerful. By the evening light the Sainte-Baume seemed to control the plain in which we stood, minimizing the lofty Gothic structure of Saint-Maximin in the foreground, and integrating the shapeless town beside the church. When you are in the streets in the town of Saint-Maximin, you are not aware of the presence of the Sainte-Baume, away there in the westward distance, the direction of Marseilles. Out in these fields, not a mile from the town's circumference, you notice first the mountain and then the church.

By screwing up my eyes I could just see the place at which the peasant's arm was pointing – a whitish patch between two blackish patches high up on the mountain's side: the cave and chapel of Saint Mary Magdalen within their frame of shrubs and trees. In this cave Mary Magdalen is reputed to have led a life of meditation, and there, according to one of the most persistent Christian traditions of Provence, she died. For centuries the legend of her life and death up there on the isolated mountain has sanctified the plain below the Sainte-Baume.

Popular belief attributes the conversion of this region of Provence to the presence of Mary Magdalen. For a variety of reasons, many of them obvious, this story, which is comparable to the Somersetshire legends of Saint Joseph of Arimathea at Glastonbury, is not likely to be true; its truth is of no real consequence. The important point is not whether certain personages mentioned in the gospels made or did not make a lengthy journey to Marseilles by boat, but the fact that the people of Provence believed for centuries that they had done so, and that this area of southern France, in many ways so pagan, has absorbed the stories of these saints into its daily life. The crypt of the great fortress-abbey of Saint-Victor at Marseilles contains an early altar dedicated to Saint Mary Magdalen. An oratory in which she was said to have prayed was still shown at Aix in the early nineteenth century. As we have seen, the conquest of the Tarasque by Saint Martha is once more annually celebrated at Tarascon beside the Rhône, while the gypsies' pilgrimage to the stalwart church of the Saintes-Maries-de-la-Mer remains as popular as in the days of Mistral. Throughout western Provence these beliefs and stories linger. They are as much a part of the Provençal countryside as the tangible vestiges – the ruined monuments and broken temples – of the rule of imperial Rome. '*On ne peut mettre le pied sur le sol de Provence sans heurter à chaque pas la mémoire de sainte Marie-Madeleine,*' wrote Lacordaire in 1860. Over what were thought to be the relics of this saint, enclosed in a Gallo-Roman sarcophagus of Arles marble, the Dominicans began to build the basilica of Saint-Maximin in the thirteenth century. Left uncompleted two hundred years later, this great church remains the only major Gothic monument in Provence.

II

Stories of Saint Mary Magdalen's activities in Provence do not seem to have been widely circulated before the tenth, or at best the ninth, century – there is again a parallel here with the date at which the Glastonbury saga of Saint Joseph of Arimathea gained currency in the west of England. Towards the end of the eleventh century – '*soit qu'il y eût bonne foi, soit qu'il y eût industrie,*' remarks Lacordaire – the monks of the hill-city of Vézelay in Burgundy declared that the body of Saint Mary Magdalen lay under the high altar of that abbey. A pilgrimage forbidden by the bishop of that diocese but subsequently authorized by the pope developed. Soon pilgrims from all over Europe were swarming towards Vézelay, which became a centre for the preaching of the Second and the Third Crusades. To explain the presence of the saint's body in Burgundy the monks of Vézelay pointed out that it had first lain at Saint-Maximin in Provence, but had been taken north for safety at the time of the Saracen invasions.

This was not a wise explanation, for it provoked a search carried out in the year of 1279 at Saint-Maximin, and resulting in the discovery of a rival body of the saint. This search, conducted in the presence of Saint Louis' nephew, Charles de Provence, ended in the finding of a sarcophagus of marble in the crypt of the old Cassianite church. Opened with great pomp in the presence of two archbishops, the sarcophagus was found to contain a skeleton, and with the skeleton a piece of bark ostensibly dated 710 and stating that the body of Saint Mary Magdalen had been removed from an alabaster coffin to this marble one, and hidden from the Saracens. At the directions of Charles de Provence the body was divided into three parts – the skull (to which a piece of apparently living flesh was still adhering) was placed in a golden reliquary with a crystal mask over the face; the right arm was enclosed in a reliquary of silver-gilt supported by four silver-gilt lions; while the rest of the skeleton was laid in a silver casket. The King of Naples and Sicily, father of Charles de Provence, sent his own jewelled crown to be placed upon the skull, which was then taken to Rome and shown to Boniface VIII. This pope gave the relics his official recognition and authorized the construction of a large church, to be looked after by the Dominican order, at Saint-Maximin in the county of Provence.

From the thirteenth century onwards, the pilgrimage to Saint-Maximin, and to the neighbouring cave of the Sainte-Baume, increased in volume and in popularity, rivalling that of Vézelay, half of whose pilgrims it drained away. Louis XI, the first king who ruled Provence as well as France, pronounced Mary Magdalen to be a French saint – 'une fille de France'. Both Charles VIII and Louis XII continued to encourage the cult. Queen Anne of Brittany sent a golden statuette of herself to be placed near the reliquary which held the holy skull. François I, Charles IX, and Louis XIII all contributed to the embellishment of the church and of the grotto; while Louis XIV was the last reigning French monarch to pay homage in person at les Saints Lieux de Provence. The monastery attached to the church became exceedingly prosperous and continued so until the outbreak of the Revolution, when it was shut. In 1793 the chapel of the Sainte-Baume in the mountain was destroyed on the orders of Barras, but the church, though pillaged and scheduled for demolition, was saved. A rather dubious Provençal tradition ascribes the saving of the church to Lucien Bonaparte, then resident in 'Marathon' (the Revolutionary name for Saint-Maximin) and married to the innkeeper's sister. According to his own story, given in his memoirs, 'Brutus' Bonaparte saved many of the Saint-Maximinois and their wives from the guillotine at Orange. He does not mention the church (which he is supposed to have saved by ordering it to be used as a warehouse) while the general tone of his memoirs certainly suggests that had he indeed preserved this building he would have drawn attention to this fact. Subsequently auctioned as national property, the basilica was bought quite cheaply by a Madame Tan, who returned it to the Church authorities at the Restoration. In 1859 it was bought back by the Dominicans, an order just revived in France. It was at this moment, and because of this re-purchase, that the church of Saint-Maximin and its rather misty traditions inspired the most popular of the written words of the great leader of the Dominican revival, the preacher Lacordaire.

III

The son of a bourgeois family in the Burgundian countryside near Châtillon-sur-Seine, Lacordaire passed an agnostic youth in Dijon and in Paris, was converted at the age of twenty-one in 1823, and was ordained priest by the Archbishop of Paris four years later. At first connected with the *Avenir* movement of his friends Montalembert and Lamennais, he had withdrawn from it at the first signs of papal disapproval, and in 1835 had been invited by the archbishop to preach from the pulpit of Notre Dame. For the next two years his sermons drew all Paris; his success was as fashionable as that of F. D. Maurice in mid-Victorian London, but also far more widespread. In 1837 he relinquished his appointment at Notre Dame, withdrew to Rome, and was there received with two of his countrymen into the order of the friars of Saint Dominic, an order which had been suppressed in France at the Revolution and had not been revived. The remainder of Lacordaire's life (save for the few days in 1848 in which he functioned as a member of the Chamber of Deputies) was divided between his preaching (he resumed his *conférences* at Notre Dame in 1843) and his carefully planned campaign to reinstate the Dominicans throughout the length and breadth of France. In the autobiographical fragment which he dictated as he lay dying he describes the stages by which the Dominicans had been reinstated in that country – the first small house at Nancy, the second establishment in the deserted convent of Chalais near Grenoble, the third at Flavigny not far from Dijon, the fourth in Paris, and so on. In September 1859 this steady infiltration culminated in the solemn re-entry of the Dominicans into the famous monastery and austere basilica of Saint-Maximin-la-Sainte-Baume. To celebrate this climax of his life's work, and try to revive the pilgrimages to *les Saints Lieux de Provence*, Lacordaire sat down and composed the best known of his writings, *La Vie de Sainte-Marie-Madeleine*.

Even in his own day, Lacordaire's sermons were criticized for their lack of logic and faulty reasoning; no one tried to deny their extraordinary emotional power. The same criticisms have been levelled at his book on Saint Mary Magdalen, for he accepted every story of her presence in Provence without hesitation, and even openly regretted that the '*Noli me tangere*', the piece of skin upon the skull at Saint-Maximin which was said to be the mark of the hand of Christ, had been lost in the eighteenth century. Today this excessive credulity seems as unimportant as that of the Provençaux themselves, for the *Vie de Sainte-Marie-Madeleine* can be read with enjoyment for two quite extraneous reasons – the magnificent disquisition upon the sublimity of friendship, and the descriptive passages on the Sainte-Baume and on Provence.

The works of the great often abound in beauties of which the authors themselves may well have been quite unaware. Just as you may read Carlyle for the shimmering gem-like portraits of his contemporaries with which his prose works are studded, so you may read Lacordaire for his descriptions of French scenery instead of for his Christian apologetics. Born and brought up in the same landscape as Lamartine, Lacordaire had a similar passion for the French countryside and a similar sensibility towards its perfections. His account (in his autobiography) of the ruined monastery at Chalais forms a fine example of his descriptive gifts; these he applied with an especial passion to Provence. His certainty that a saint whom he venerated had lived and died in this southern land gave impetus to his natural enthusiasm for a country which he compared to some promontory of Greece or Italy thrust out towards the Mediterranean, *'cette mer qui baigne tous les rivages fameux'*. With certain creative natures, as with certain lovers, the actual truth or value of that by which they are inspired is of secondary importance, the essential factor being the strength and the expression of the emotions which are thus released.

Good landscape writing, like good landscape painting, makes public a personal interpretation of the place portrayed, and thus enhances the general appreciation of it, providing, as it were, a new lens through which others can look. Provence, which has been so much painted, provides numerous instances of this – what van Gogh did for Arles, what Cézanne did for the environs of Aix, or Corot for Avignon and for Villeneuve. Now, you cannot place Lacordaire, a fine preacher and a compelling spiritual force, but a sentimental writer, on a level with any of these; yet his descriptions of the view from the terrace of the Sainte-Baume, looking down towards Saint-Maximin, and of the country round the church and monastery shed a kind of lustre on these landscapes as soft and warm as the light of a summer evening in the Var. A strange excitement throbs through these passages. And who has more exactly caught the sudden shock of that intoxicating experience – a first entry into Provence? *'Lorsque le voyageur descend les pentes du Rhône,'* he writes, *'à un certain moment, sur la gauche, les montagnes s'écartent, l'horizon s'élargit, le ciel devient plus pur, la terre plus somptueuse, l'air plus doux; c'est la Provence.'*

IV

If you approach Saint-Maximin from Draguignan, as I did, it seems a loose and undistinguished-looking place. Draguignan, a hill-town with a barracks in it, has steeply tilted streets as narrow as a coffin. Saint-Maximin is wide and flat. It is a very small town, to most intents and purposes a village. An air of impermanence, even of makeshift, hovers uncertainly about the central square. It seems a town in which people change buses, but do not stay to live. At one end of the *place* (inevitably called the Boulevard Jean-Jaurès) are trees, and under the trees, benches. There is also an eighteenth-century fountain with a stiff obelisk above it. On to the obelisk is jammed a clumsy four-faced clock. The main hotel is a crouching, comfortable building with shrubs in painted pots outside its windows, and to the right of the doorway a long kitchen in which big copper saucepans give forth an orange glint. Saint-Maximin has all the qualities one might associate with a pilgrim town.

'Saint-Maximin,' wrote Prosper Mérimée from the inn there, in September 1834, 'est un misérable trou entre Aix et Draguignan.' He was forced to spend the night in the town, since he could get no horses to take him back to Aix. His visit to Saint-Maximin took up one day of a four-month tour of the monuments, libraries and museums of the Midi, a part of his regular duties as Inspector-General of the Historical Monuments of France. Mérimée was at this time thirty-one and already well known. He was a quiet, furtive-looking young man, with small sharp eyes and a disagreeable expression. He detested his journeys in the provinces, and would describe himself in letters to his friends as 'victimized' by the provincials, who treated him as a celebrity as well as an official, bored him with their egotism and their coin collections, and exhausted him with long climbs in church belfries and walks uphill to see some 'prehistoric' stone. He had not been in Provence before this visit, and he found the inns particularly nasty. He said they smelt of oil and garlic, that there were rats in the bedrooms and bugs in the beds. The roads, along which he jolted in a succession of carts, carriages and pony-traps, were atrocious. The conditions in which educated, upper-class people lived in towns such as Arles or Avignon amazed him – their houses squeezed in between a busy laundry and a tannery stinking of raw hides, and their front doors swinging open on to squalid ill-paved streets. As we have seen, he came to the conclusion that what this part of France needed was dictatorship.

In August Mérimée had been to Vézelay – a church at that time still untouched by Viollet-le-Duc – and now he was come to see the alternative sepulchre of Mary Magdalen. In his private letters he expressed great disappointment at the uncompleted state of the great church. 'Il y a une grande église,' he wrote to Jenny Dacquin, 'à laquelle il ne manque qu'une façade, des tours, un clocher et autres menus details. Je me suis laissé prendre à ce regular humbug et je ne *puis sortir de Saint-Maximin faute de chevaux.*' In his *Notes d'un voyage dans le Midi de la France*, Mérimée was more lenient to Saint-Maximin. He admitted that its local celebrity was well justified by its size and by the height of the three naves and the elegance of the apse, though he could not resist a gibe at the absence of a west front. In contrast to the abbey at Vézelay, which he had found almost derelict, the church at Saint-Maximin was well looked after. He was impressed by the '*belle teinte sombre*' of the interior, very noticeable at an epoch in which every church in France was being white-washed, and he found that it was only the personal courage of the curé which had saved the church from the painters' hands. When they had arrived with their buckets and brushes, Père Logier had locked the doors of the church, preferring temporarily to excommunicate the inhabitants of Saint-Maximin rather than see the church's interior spoiled. Mérimée, who had been waging a lonely fight against the prevailing pious bad taste, held him up as an example of aesthetic wisdom. He said, too, that it was the curé who was responsible for the perfect state of the famous seventeenth-century choir-stalls of Saint-Maximin which, like the Louis Quinze pulpit and the rococo stucco work over the high altar, were as clean as they could be. Père Logier cleaned and polished all the woodwork himself – 'Do you think,' he asked his visitor, 'that I would let ignorant hands touch these beautiful things?' Mérimée was so much taken with the priest's zeal and intelligence that when he sat down that night to write a report to his Minister, he asked him to send a picture to Saint-Maximin. '*Il n'y a pas une église en France qui soit plus digne de recevoir des objets d'art,*' he commented.

Praise from Prosper Mérimée was rare.

V

The exterior appearance of Saint-Maximin has changed little in the hundred and eighteen years since Mérimée's visit. Perhaps it is the fact that there are no other great Gothic buildings in south Provence that makes this vast basilica seem so chilling and so pale. Around and above the great west door the walls rise grey and raw. Between the cracks of the unfinished masonry sturdy green plants are sprouting, to strain and quiver as the mistral blows. The chain of saints on the west door was hacked flat at the time of the French Revolution. Their ovoid, featureless faces and sliced-off limbs seem somehow in character with the uncompleted state of the façade. North of the church, at right angles to it, stands the Hôtel de Ville, a pretty seventeenth-century *pavillon* which once formed part of the monastic precincts. The monastery itself, lying between church and *pavillon*, has been somewhat reconstructed in the nineteenth century and now houses Lacordaire's Dominicans. Aquiline and tonsured, these friars stride about the streets of the town in their white serge habits, their abruptly energetic movements hampered by their skirts. At the east end of the church are some farm stables, and on the south, opposite the monastery, is a miniature dusty square, presided over by a strong plane tree. On the July morning when I went to see the basilica, a haywain stood against one wall of the square. It stood there in the shadow, as though sheltering from the heat. For the heat, like the silence round the church, was total, and as so often in Provence the heat seemed fierce and the silence sinister. Far up over the roof some swallows circled and dipped across the buttresses.

Inside, the basilica is unkempt and damp. There are few more melancholy sights in Provence than the present condition of this splendid church, in which the severity of the Gothic nave was once relieved by a great wealth of showy baroque work – the choir-stalls carved in 1692, the pulpit, the organ-case, the frieze of plaster cherubim over the altar. All these objects are still in place, but all dilapidated. The woodwork is worm-eaten, and the gilded stucco crumbling and mildewed, falling in dirty flakes upon the chancel floor. An interesting Renaissance altarpiece, painted for the church in 1520, and containing the first recorded view of the Palais des Papes at Avignon, is so filthy that you can scarcely see it. The praise which Prosper Mérimée bestowed upon the curé of 1834 would certainly not be merited by the modern sacristan, or the monks now responsible for the upkeep and the preservation of this church. The basilica seems, indeed, to be in much the same state as when Lacordaire wrote of it in 1859, 'debout encore, mais pauvre, nu, désolé, tout couvert des cicatrices du siècle qui s'est plu aux ruines, comme les autres s'étaient plus dans l'édification'. For Lacordaire's campaign to revive the popularity of *les Saints Lieux de Provence* has not outlived his century. That century, in any case, provided Catholic France with new saints of its own. The medieval cult of Mary Magdalen, the repentant sinner, gave way to that of the schoolchild Bernadette at Lourdes or the nun Thérèse at Lisieux. Only within Provence itself has devotion to the Sainte-Baume survived. Its centre is still the crypt of the church of Saint-Maximin. You enter this crypt by a steep, short flight of steps in the north transept.

This crypt of Saint-Maximin is even more cramped than most. What space there is in it seems taken up by four fine Gallo-Roman sarcophagi, probably of Arlesian origin, which have low bas-reliefs carved along their sides. These sarcophagi are those unearthed in 1279 by Charles de Provence, and since then officially regarded as the receptacles of the bodies of Mary Magdalen, Maximin, Sidonia and Trophimus. At the end of the crypt is an illuminated niche protected by a sheet of glass. Behind the glass, and on the shelf, stands an ormolu head of a woman with long hair, over life-size. The face of this reliquary, which, made in 1860, replaces the thirteenth-century one lost in the Revolution, can be removed like a lid, and lies propped against the wall of the niche. This arrangement reveals a brittle, brownish skull, which contrasts sharply with the bland and Second Empire features of the golden face beside it. This is the skull which has been regarded for seven centuries as that of Saint Mary Magdalen.

To Lacordaire this little crypt was 'the third most important tomb in Christendom'. To the sceptical church historian Duchesne it was a typical burial-vault of some rich local family of the fifth or sixth century. The arguments for and against the authenticity of the relics have never been concluded. One can assume that they never will be. The only thing that seems fairly certain is that this skull, together with a finger and some fragments of vertebrae, did once form part of a female body disinterred in the thirteenth century, and subsequently reverenced by pilgrims from all over Europe. Whose body it was, no one can tell, and why should this matter? For those dead bones did more than inspire Lacordaire. They were, in a most literal sense, responsible for the building of the great basilica itself.

To students of Provence, Saint-Maximin has another and a purely accidental relevance. For it was here that the Emperor Napoleon pronounced his final verdict on the Provençaux. Quoting the narrative of Count Waldbourg-Truchses, one of the Allied Commissioners who went with the ex-Emperor to Elba in 1814, Chateaubriand has preserved the story of Napoleon's alarm on entering Provence. As the cavalcade of carriages had journeyed southwards, the attitude of the people in the villages and towns along the route began to change. It was on the frontiers of Provence that Napoleon first met open threats and insults. At Plan d'Organ and on the outskirts of Avignon the Emperor, who had had to disguise himself, had shown some fear. When they reached Saint-Maximin – the town in which his brother Lucien had been married twenty years earlier – Napoleon, now dressed in Austrian uniform, summoned the *sous-préfet* of Aix who was in the town. He upbraided him. He told him he should blush to see the Austrian uniform, and to know that this was his ex-sovereign's only means of protection against the people of Provence. 'C'est une méchante race que les Provençaux,' said Napoleon, 'Ils ont commis toutes sortes d'horreurs et de crimes dans la Révolution et sont prêts à recommencer; mais quand il s'agit de se battre avec courage, alors ce sont des lâches.' Provence, he added, had never given him one regiment of which he could be proud.

Although Napoleon's outburst need not be taken too literally (he was harassed and persecuted when he made it), its implication that the Provençaux are a race apart from other Frenchmen, and a violent and potentially cruel people, will seem valid to those who have done much travelling in Provence. 'Foreigners think this is a gentle country, but in reality it is harsh and fierce,' a man once said to me at Les Baux. It is indeed a bitter and ferocious country, full of violence and lethargy, perfidy and good nature, full of every contradiction under its burning sun. The pride and respect with which the turbulent country people hold the memory of Saint Mary Magdalen seems merely one more example of this contradiction – for what tale could be more tranquil, what ideal more calm and gentle than that of this slow life of meditation and this quiet death in a grotto on the Sainte-Baume?

Less macabre than the Magdalen's blackened skull, in its helmet of glittering silver-gilt, is the reliquary bust of another early saint, preserved in a Gothic church amongst the shady hills above the valley of the river Argens, some fifteen miles north of Saint-Maximin. Said to contain the relics of Saint Marcellus, a fourth-century pope and martyr famous for the severity of his edicts against lapsed Christians, this painted reliquary, in form the head and shoulders of a solemn-looking mitred ecclesiastic with widely staring eyes, is kept in a twilit sanctuary of the fifteenth-century church of Barjols, behind a sheet of glass. Annually, on the January feast-day of Saint Marcellus, it is withdrawn from its dim alcove and exposed at evening, on the large square before the church. Here it presides each year over the ceremonial blessing, followed by the ceremonial slaughter, of a garlanded ox. The carcass of the animal is then carried in procession through the streets attended by the clergy, the butchers and the cooks of Barjols; while it is later being roasted whole, the people of the town dance round it to the sound of rustic flutes, tambourines, and volleys of musketry. The ox is then cut up and distributed next day to the poor. Clearly of pagan origin, this striking festival must long ago have been incorporated by the Church into the celebrations in honour of the saint whose bones the town of Barjols shelters.

I have never yet been to Barjols in midwinter, on the feast of Saint Marcellus, but each time I have passed through the town, in high summer and in autumn, I have fallen under the charm of this seductive place, called, so a guide-book tells us, 'the Tivoli of Provence'. With its romantic, Morland-like scenery of overhanging trees and rushing torrents, quivering reeds and fresh hill meadows of bright grass, Barjols is in fact one of the loveliest towns in the whole lovely department of the Var.

Situated high in the hills to the north-east of Saint-Maximin, Barjols stands – or rather, so haphazard are its houses on the hillside, seems to fall – at the junction of a picturesque small river named (like rivers in the French West Indies) Eau Salée, and a wild torrent called Des Écrevisses. By trade Barjols is a town of tanneries, and it is partly the effect of the weatherboard warehouses and little factories of these, partly the abandoned quality of the rocky but leaf-laden scenery, that reminds you, at first sight, of a town in southern Norway. But once you have entered Barjols, you recognize how much it is purely Provençal. I had stopped there on various occasions, usually to change buses on the way from Saint-Maximin across the lavender-fields of the Durance valley to Manosque. These brief glimpses had made me want to linger there, and so one September when I happened to have a car I took the opportunity of staying at Barjols on a long round-about itinerary from the coast near Toulon up to Saint-Rémy and Les Baux, by way of Brignoles, where are preserved the gloves, the mitre and dalmatic of Saint Louis of Anjou, the secluded abbey of La Celle with its grim, Italian crucified Christ, Saint-Maximin and Silvacane. Since it was autumn, the grape-picking was in full swing, and country carts laden with crimson grapes were crawling down the roads. In the vineyards by the seashore near Toulon the vine-pickers were still working in the evening as we passed. Their sunburnt faces black beneath their hats of yellow straw, they moved through the vineyards in bobbing herds, not unlike the motion of goats. We took the road up into the mountains, by Solliés-Pont, Puget-Ville and the hamlet of Forcal-quairet, a road which soon becomes little more than a dust-track twisting up a deserted valley, along a hillside silver-white with olive trees, and stepped into shallow terraces at some epoch now remote. As the sun set the sky became tangerine colour, with the mountains carefully outlined against it; but as darkness fell a new glow lit the mountain tops, for a forest fire was blazing mysteriously away on one of them, making a crater of flame ringed by thick smoke. By the time we reached Saint-Maximin it was night, and after a *pastis* in a swarming workmen's bar near the church there, we set off by the light of the headlamps up the winding road to Barjols, along the Argens. By daylight so idyllic, this road seemed insidious by night, leading one up and up into the cold green hills, away, as it seemed, from warmth and life. When we reached Barjols, we found it in a state of great excitement over the arrival of a conjurer who gave a most lively and ingenious performance in the main café of the town. The conjurer was called Pinkerton. His female assistant, who sat behind a screen, was Madame Nelly.

The next morning, in sparkling autumn sunshine, I went out to explore Barjols. The sights of the town are few. They consist of the fifteenth-century church with its relics of 'Saint Marcel'; the elaborate Renaissance doorway, ornamented with love-motifs, of the old town house of the family of Pontevès, whose ruined château is to be seen in a village two miles away; a huge moss-grown fountain in a narrow, steeply sloping *place* near the church, and which rivals those of Salon and of Aix; and a plane tree of gigantic girth claiming to be the largest plane tree in Provence. The church, which you enter by going down two or three steps, is cold and gloomy. It contains nothing of interest apart from the reliquary bust, above a small fourteenth-century sarcophagus, in Saint Marcellus' shrine. In no sense a work of art, this head, gazing out from the shadows of the chapel with unwinking eyes, seems, behind its glass panel, to be in some rigid and unpleasant way alive. The expression on the painted face is severe, even ferocious. Lacking that air of peace and resignation which one senses in the reliquary masks and withered corpses crowned with paper flowers of some saints' bodies in Italian churches, Saint Marcellus is as alarming to confront suddenly as are the throngs of staring waxworks in the Musée Arlatan at Arles. It is not a figure to inspire devotion in the most pious persons, and I left the church hurriedly, returning with relief to the hot square and the sun.

The Hôtel de Pontevès is in the lower part of the town and hard to find. I was finally directed to it by some handsome washerwomen scrubbing linen in a fountain nearby. In a neglected, indeed even a dilapidated state, the house seems at present to be enduring some form of restoration, no doubt under the assiduous and energetic care of the Beaux Arts. Doors had been taken off their hinges, workmen were busy at the walls, and the inner court was a cloud of white cement and stone dust. The large arched doorway, between flat Renaissance pilasters, is decorated with a frieze and some medallions, notable work both for their fine detail and the merry, erotic character of their subjects. There is, however, little else to detain one at the Hôtel de Pontevès, and I soon returned to the more celebrated fountain of Barjols, a moss-grown vase of stone from which water oozes, and which, from its position in a charming little sloping *place*, is as picturesque as its prototype, the warm fountain in the Cours Mirabeau at Aix, is ugly. Close to the fountain stands the giant plane tree, nine metres in circumference, and evidently one of the largest specimens of its kind on earth. On one side of the same little *place* (which is in fact little more than a paved street) is the tiny Hôtel de Ville of Barjols, with an iron balcony and a limp tricolour over the door. Across the way from the Hôtel de Ville is a small, agreeable restaurant, Le Logis de la Fontaine, where one can lunch or dine at a first-floor window, and gaze down at the lazy-looking, moss-grown fountain, and at the fat trunk and sturdy branches of the biggest plane tree in Provence.

CHAPTER TEN

I

THAT ILLUSION OF SPACE, THAT SENSE of being surrounded by a limitless horizon, which are the first impressions that the English receive when, having disembarked the motor-car at Le Touquet or Dieppe, they set off to drive deeply into France, are perhaps most potent on a journey through Provence. In France you are always more conscious of the sky than you are in England; and in the south the light, as crystal clear as the fabled light of Greece, gives special brilliance to the wide variety of landscapes which compose the Provençal scene. This variety is indeed immense, and we may fancy that no other area in France of size equivalent to that of Provence can offer such sudden and breath-taking visual changes. Turner, who spent some weeks wandering in Provence on his way to Rome in September 1828, and suffered abominably from the heat, found this variety his only comfort: 'I must see the south of France,' he wrote,* 'which almost knocked me up, the heat was so intense, particularly at Nîmes and Avignon; and until I got a plunge into the sea at Marseilles, I felt so weak that nothing but the change of scene kept me onwards to my distant point.' It is this constant change of scene which, as I have tried to show, forms one of the chief pleasures of travel in Provence. There are such splendid, abrupt contrasts as that between the plain of Saint-Rémy and Maillane, with the cypress screens, the sheltered vines and flowering orchards and nursery gardens on the one hand, and the neighbouring barren heights of Les Baux on the other. There is the contrast between the wooded foothills about Aix, and the stark, eagle-haunted pinnacles of rock above Moustiers-Sainte-Marie. There is the contrast between valleys such as that in which Vauvenargues or Apt is situated, and the flat,

---

*J. M. W. Turner to G. Jones, Rome, 13 October 1828, quoted in A. J. Finberg's *The Life of J. M. W. Turner, R.A.* (Oxford, 1939).

burnished land of the Camargue with its wild flamingoes and its solitary farmsteads. The sea coast, where it remains unspoiled, offers a similar range of contrast – the difference, let us say, between the *calanques* of the Marseilleveyre, those strange sea-creeks outside Marseilles in which we can imagine pirates' long-boats hiding, and the pure Odyssean beauty of the peninsula of Giens and the islands of Porquerolles. Provence offers scenery of every period.

For when Lady Blessington complained that the country about Avignon was 'uninteresting' she was unconsciously stating the fact that landscapes can be classified into periods, and have often been judged by purely period taste. Some landscapes, that is to say, seem, as it were, arranged for the Romantics; some are strictly classical; some medieval; some modern. Sisteron, one of the most northerly bastions of Provence, on the confines of the Dauphiné, and built below a jutting rock on which its citadel is placed at the swirling junction of the Durance and the Bléonne, is the sort of city Lady Blessington's contemporaries most authentically admired, and which Turner painted, wreathed in summer mist. Les Baux, and the bleak, lunar road that leads to it, is surely, as Robida remarked, a landscape drawn by Gustave Doré. Vaison-la-Romaine, with its baths, Roman theatre, temple and antique statues, seems as Roman, as classical, as anything in metropolitan Italy. If you look at Tarascon from Beaucaire upon the Rhône's opposite bank you see the castle of King René mirrored in the river water, a sight almost too picturesque for us to bear; but when you look at Beaucaire from Tarascon you see not the corresponding castle only, but the great suspension bridge that spans the river, and, to the left, the tall chimneys of a giant power-station give a contemporary vitality to this traditional scene.

The task of singling out a landscape for description is even more invidious than that of choosing monuments and towns. Each traveller in Provence will make his own discoveries and stick to them, forming and carrying away from the countryside his own mental pictures, not those of any guide. But all the same there are certain views not widely noted, which should be signalled and might otherwise be missed. In my own mind there is at least one that ranks with the prospect from Les Baux, or the river-valley of the Gardon seen from the viaduct of the Pont du Gard, or the seashore of Hyères, or the plain of Avignon seen from the lilac-coloured Alpilles beyond the Plateau des Antiques at Saint-Rémy. This is the view downwards from the summit of a high conical hill round which the battered township of Forcalquier, sacked repeatedly throughout its history, still valiantly clings. This view best falls within the category that I have called 'medieval landscape', for all its elements combine to form the prototype of a country scene in some French primitive, with grey rocks, smooth sloping meadows on sharp hillsides, corn-stooks like witches' hats, bulbous trees, and little figures working in the fields. With the dramatically placed citadel of Sisteron, and with Digne upon the river Bléonne, Forcalquier is unquestionably among the most beautiful (and, I believe, least visited) places in the whole hard mountain region of Upper Provence, the department of the Basses-Alpes. From Saint-Maximin and Barjols this town is easily reached by way of its next-door neighbour, the hill-station of Manosque.

II

In summer-time the northward drive from Barjols to Manosque and the other towns of the Durance valley is especially enjoyable, since the road soon leaves the shady copses of the Argens to emerge into the open, treeless, sandy uplands studded with a profusion of the grey-green lavender plants which form a local industry in this part of Provence. But it is something of a shock to leave the scented heights of Valensole, Tavernes and Varages, and to come slowly down into the country of the wide, pale Durance river, here the colour of buttermilk, and in summer-time dry and sluggish in its stony bed. To southwards factory chimneys are steaming in the haze, and an extremely long and ugly iron bridge takes you across the river into the garish suburbs of Manosque, a medieval town, which has replaced its old ramparts by an encircling boulevard, and is built up the side of a hill. Considered a good resort for the tuber-cular, Manosque is a town in which you notice first the bus-station, the garages, the bars and cafés with their fruit-machines, the tele-graph wires which are woven like a web about the fine old gate. This gate, called 'la Porte de la Saunerie', has been preserved even though the town's walls are demolished. Crowned by an iron cage, it now serves as belfry to the town. The objects of interest to the casual visitor to Manosque comprise this old gate, and another of the same date at the other end of the town; one or two private hôtels of the mid eighteenth century; a war memorial of more than permissible ugliness and size; and Notre Dame de Romigier, a small black Madonna and child, doll-like in their stiff, white embroidered clothes, enshrined in the Lady Chapel of the main church of Manosque and illuminated by the sunshine filtering through some azure glass, so that the figures seem floating in a supernatural turquoise light. Manosque has enthusiastic devotees who go there yearly from the towns and cities of lower Provence. I may have been prejudiced on my two visits, but I confess I could see no reason to loiter in this town instead of pushing on up the Durance valley towards the northern borders of Provence.

The second mightiest river in Provence, the Durance, is, in aspect and in character, very unlike the Rhône with which it merges below Avignon. Rising in the mysterious regions of the High Alps of the Dauphiné, and strengthened by the tributary torrents of the Buech, the Bléonne and the Asse, the Durance rages through the gorges of Sisteron to enter Provence. Here it is a violent and tumultuous river, but by the time it reaches Manosque, and still more so farther westward where it forms the tame boundary between the two departments of the Vaucluse and the Bouches-du-Rhône, it is a wide, uneventful-looking river with none of the dramatic appearance and the solemn majesty of the Rhône. But if you follow the motor-road upriver from Manosque, the valley scenery becomes wilder and more romantic. It is from this motor-road that a detour should be made to Forcalquier.

The drive from Manosque to Forcalquier is devious. Long before you reach your destination you see the town lying before you, built around the lower slopes of a high conical hill which is covered with dark trees and capped by a cupola. This cupola, which, with the sharp trim hill, the biscuit colour of the town, and the fresh green of the fields about it, makes you think you are in Umbria, turns out, on close examination, to belong to a nineteenth-century chapel erected on the site of a fort which used to occupy the summit of the hill and was dismantled during the Wars of Religion. So steep is the hill on which Forcalquier stands that the road approaches it in terraced stages; on one side of the road a string of houses, shops and cafés stands well below road level, on the other side more shops are built upon a high embankment faced with stone. This winding road conducts you to the spacious central square, a place usually as empty as a deserted parade-ground, and entirely dominated by a great Romanesque cathedral, which has suffered, like the town itself, from generations of invasions and civil wars. Before the cathedral is an old fountain, with a modern plaque upon it commemorating the marriage of Henry III of England with Eleanor of Provence, whose father held the countship of this town.

The cathedral of Forcalquier has a rude and elementary grandeur about it comparable to that of the great Roman ruins of Provence, and seeming, like them, a kind of natural phenomenon. Outside it is as powerful and impressive as is a first sight of some great English Norman cathedral; inside it is remarkable only for two particularly delicate Gothic chapels in the style usually confined to the churches of the Île-de-France, and seldom met with in Provence. These chapels are at present obscured by modern frescos, and the whole church, like that of Saint-Maximin, is in a state of considerable neglect. Unlike Saint-Maximin, however, the cathedral of Forcalquier seems the centre of its little town, integrated into it in a way that the Gothic basilica of Saint Mary Magdalen is not related to that pilgrim town. Forcalquier, which consists of narrow crumbling streets like the back streets of Draguignan or those of the *vieille ville* of Vaison or Hyères, and one other square containing a lovely and ornate fifteenth-century fountain surmounted by a figure of Saint Michael, is also a quieter place than Saint-Maximin, having the air of being depopulated, and curiously silent, even dead, by night.

To gain the top of the hill above the town you have to clamber up a lane of ruinous hovels, until you reach the half-wild shrubberies of a sombre public garden. Pushing your way on through brambles and thick undergrowth you then emerge upon a small plateau ornamented by a few fir trees, and with roots of wild lavender underfoot. A stone parapet surrounds this place, which also contains a modern chapel, and one of those marble *tables d'orientation* which gives you the names and heights of all the mountains visible on the horizon, and tells you that the hilltop is two thousand feet above the level of the distant sea. Some of the mountains on the horizon – the Lubéron, the Sainte-Baume – are identifiable without the table's help. In the foreground and the middle distance lie steep green hills with tilted fields along them. On the summer evening on which I first visited Forcalquier these fields were being scythed; in one of them this process was half-completed, others were finished, with their corn-stooks marshalled in long, curving lines. Grey geese were waddling in procession through a meadow far below, and in some of the fields farm-people were at work. On a fresh green hummock in the very centre of this landscape stood a small white Romanesque chapel, now used as a storage-house for grain.

III

When a traveller in Provence has gone as far north as Forcalquier, it would be wrong not to go farther still – say to Digne, a sad, secluded little mountain town wedged between bleak mountain-sides which keep it in perpetual shadow, or to Sisteron, an ancient border stronghold severely damaged in the late war.

Digne is not a place in which you want to stay for long, nor is it a town in which a stranger is likely to feel at ease or happy. The mountains close it in too grimly, and the chief feature of the town, the Cours Gassendi, called after the seventeenth-century priest and philosopher who lived and died at Digne, is a broad, dusty street of no aesthetic merit or pretensions. At one end of the Cours Gassendi, almost beyond the limits of the town, stands a fine yellow Romanesque church, Notre-Dame du Bourg, now used only for funerals, and cheek by jowl with the workyards of monumental masons, piled with great blocks of polished granite, bead wreaths and those mourning photographs of the deceased always to be found in French and Italian cemeteries. It also seems characteristic of Digne that the best position in the town is occupied by the chief prison of the Department of the Basses-Alpes, which is indeed so beautifully placed that it makes one long to commit a crime. I have been twice to Digne, and each time I disliked it, though in justice to the town I should point out that Monsieur Vaudoyer has devoted some passages of great charm to the town itself and to Gassendi in his *Beautés de la Provence*. I sat reading this book on the terrace below the church in the *haute ville* one sunny morning, but even this did not reconcile me to Digne; and I was soon driven from an agreeable bench beneath a plane tree by the suffocating sooty fumes of a chimney on fire in the town below.

Digne should be visited, if not for long; Sisteron, at the junction of the river Durance with its more tempestuous tributary, the Buech, is a town few people could resist. The two rivers mingle their dim waters about a promontory of land, on which an old country house is half-hidden in a shroud of trees. High above the town there looms a crag into which the great medieval fortress of Sisteron was incorporated; the bombing of 1944 has revealed unsuspected dungeons hollowed, like the houses at Les Baux, out of the natural rock. A stiff climb to the topmost ramparts of this ruined castle rewards you with a view as fine as that from the hilltop at Forcalquier, but far more dramatic, for on one side of Sisteron you look down into the Dauphiné, on the other into Provence. The turgid junction of the two rivers above the old stone bridge leading to the quarter called La Baume is an imposing sight, while the town of Sisteron, hemmed in between the harsh grey rocks and the rivers' banks, looks brittle and untidy. The buckled roofs of orange tiles upon the housetops are here as bright as elsewhere in Provence. These old tiles form indeed one of the most constant and characteristic elements of any tour through the country: the tiled roofs of the backstreets of Avignon, seen from the papal bedchamber; the rooftops of Vaison shimmering in the heat of June; the rooftops of the port of Martigues, of isolated cabins in the countryside round Aix, of the village of Maillane and the town of Saint-Rémy. I have already suggested that one's chief memories of a journey through Provence are colour memories: and I realized this once more as I stood looking down at the Durance and at Sisteron, for the elms, poplars and even the fresh oak trees along the rivers' banks showed dark against the startling applegreen of the water-meadows, and the faultless blue of the sky. Standing there I thought, as I had thought when seeing Provence for the first time through a grimy railway-carriage window, that it is a country that needs to be interpreted by painting rather than by writing. But while I cannot say with Robert Louis Stevenson: 'I was only happy once – that was at Hyères,' I have passed some of the happiest days of my life wandering in Provence. That happiness experienced, that pleasure and interest to be found there, are the reasons for the writing of this book.

It was a keen and windy day of early spring that I explored the debris of the castle of Sisteron. On a grassy slope below the entrance gate two bare-legged boys were wrestling, beside a tethered goat: from the upper ramparts you saw everything – the boys, the goat, the fields, the oak trees, the houses of Sisteron – foreshortened. It was afternoon, and no one was stirring in the town below. Up amongst these ruins you had a sense of loneliness and desolation, which the great extent and splendour of the view only enhanced.

This noble, rock-bound panorama was not the sunny, the smiling Provence of foreign legend. This was a fierce, sad, formidable country, as uneasy as the wind that was blustering across the ramparts and straining, above my head in the roofless castle chapel, the ropes and stanchions of a great bronze bell.

INDEX OF PLACES

FOR THE BEST IN PAPERBACKS, LOOK FOR THE 🐧

In every corner of the world, on every subject under the sun, Penguin represents quality and variety – the very best in publishing today.

For complete information about books available from Penguin – including Puffins, Penguin Classics and Arkana – and how to order them, write to us at the appropriate address below. Please note that for copyright reasons the selection of books varies from country to country.

In the United Kingdom: Please write to *Dept E.P., Penguin Books Ltd, Harmondsworth, Middlesex, UB7 0DA.*

If you have any difficulty in obtaining a title, please send your order with the correct money, plus ten per cent for postage and packaging, to *PO Box No 11, West Drayton, Middlesex*

In the United States: Please write to *Dept BA, Penguin, 299 Murray Hill Parkway, East Rutherford, New Jersey 07073*

In Canada: Please write to *Penguin Books Canada Ltd, 2801 John Street, Markham, Ontario L3R 1B4*

In Australia: Please write to the *Marketing Department, Penguin Books Australia Ltd, P.O. Box 257, Ringwood, Victoria 3134*

In New Zealand: Please write to the *Marketing Department, Penguin Books (NZ) Ltd, Private Bag, Takapuna, Auckland 9*

In India: Please write to *Penguin Overseas Ltd, 706 Eros Apartments, 56 Nehru Place, New Delhi, 110019*

In the Netherlands: Please write to *Penguin Books Netherlands B.V., Postbus 195, NL–1380AD Weesp*

In West Germany: Please write to *Penguin Books Ltd, Friedrichstrasse 10–12, D–6000 Frankfurt/Main 1*

In Spain: Please write to *Alhambra Longman S.A., Fernandez de la Hoz 9, E–28010 Madrid*

In Italy: Please write to *Penguin Italia s.r.l., Via Como 4, I-20096 Pioltello (Milano)*

In France: Please write to *Penguin Books Ltd, 39 Rue de Montmorency, F-75003 Paris*

In Japan: Please write to *Longman Penguin Japan Co Ltd, Yamaguchi Building, 2–12–9 Kanda Jimbocho, Chiyoda-Ku, Tokyo 101*

FOR THE BEST IN PAPERBACKS, LOOK FOR THE 🐧

A CHOICE OF PENGUINS

Citizens Simon Schama

'The most marvellous book I have read about the French Revolution in the last fifty years' – Richard Cobb in *The Times*. 'He has chronicled the vicissitudes of that world with matchless understanding, wisdom, pity and truth, in the pages of this huge and marvellous book' – *Sunday Times*

Out of Africa Karen Blixen (Isak Dinesen)

After the failure of her coffee-farm in Kenya, where she lived from 1913 to 1931, Karen Blixen went home to Denmark and wrote this unforgettable account of her experiences. 'No reader can put the book down without some share in the author's poignant farewell to her farm' – *Observer*

In My Wildest Dreams Leslie Thomas

The autobiography of Leslie Thomas, author of *The Magic Army* and *The Dearest and the Best*. From Barnardo boy to original virgin soldier, from apprentice journalist to famous novelist, it is an amazing story. 'Hugely enjoyable' – *Daily Express*

The Winning Streak Walter Goldsmith and David Clutterbuck

Marks and Spencer, Saatchi and Saatchi, United Biscuits, GEC ... The UK's top companies reveal their formulas for success, in an important and stimulating book that no British manager can afford to ignore.

A Turn in the South V. S. Naipaul

'A supremely interesting, even poetic glimpse of a part of America foreigners either neglect or patronize' – *Guardian*. 'An extraordinary panorama' – *Daily Telegraph*. 'A fine book by a fine man, and one to be read with great enjoyment: a book of style, sagacity and wit' – *Sunday Times*

Family Susan Hill

'This chronicle of the author's struggles to produce a second child reads like an account of a passionate love affair ... Perhaps the most remarkable thing about this book ... is how exciting it is. Harder to put down than most fiction' – Ruth Rendell

THE PENGUIN TRAVEL LIBRARY – A SELECTION

Hindoo Holiday   J. R. Ackerley
The Flight of Ikaros   Kevin Andrews
The Innocent Anthropologist   Nigel Barley
A Curious Life for a Lady   Pat Barr
First Russia, Then Tibet   Robert Byron
Granite Island   Dorothy Carrington
An Indian Summer   James Cameron
Siren Land   Norman Douglas
Brazilian Adventure   Peter Fleming
The Hill of Devi   E. M. Forster
Too Late to Turn Back   Barbara Greene
Pattern of Islands   Arthur Grimble
Writings from Japan   Lafcadio Hearn
A Little Tour in France   Henry James
Mornings in Mexico   D. H. Lawrence
The Stones of Florence and **Venice Observed**   Mary McCarthy
They Went to Portugal   Rose Macaulay
The Colossus of Maroussi   Henry Miller
Calcutta   Geoffrey Moorhouse
Spain   Jan Morris
The Big Red Train Ride   Eric Newby
The Other Nile   Charlie Pye-Smith
The Marsh Arabs   Wilfred Thesiger
Journey into Cyprus   Colin Thubron
Ninety-Two Days   Evelyn Waugh
Maiden Voyage   Denton Welch